ENDOR

"Improving Justice on the Earth Study Guide is a must have tool for Advocates everywhere to inspire your local attorney and/or law student chapter to grow closer to God and to better serve the body of Christ."

Brent McBurney, President & CEO, Advocates International

"I have been honoured with an advance manuscript of *Improving Justice on Earth: A Summary Christian Worldview on Law, Justice and Government Study Guide*. Having practiced law on the government side since graduation as State Attorney, Judge and now as Chief Prosecutor, issues of enforcement of law and order vis a vis doing justice are daily challenges. Patrick Talbot's book will therefore go a long way in providing much needed material to legal practitioners, especially we who heed Advocates International's mantra of Doing Justice with Compassion.

This book is further evidence that the Lord is our Judge, He is our King. He is our Lawgiver. I gladly commend it to all lawyers, students of law, Legislators and public servants."

Justice Mike J. Chibita, Chief Prosecutor, DPP, Uganda
Past President, Advocates Africa

"[V]iolence is committed against millions of vulnerable people, every day, in every nation. These children, women and men deserve to be protected – but this will only happen when we choose to see them, defend them, and ensure that ethical and responsive justice systems exist at the local level. And, the good news is that this is possible! We at IJM have seen that when laws are enforced, violent criminals are stopped, the poor are protected, and families can flourish in safer communities. *The Improving Justice on the Earth Study Guide* will help you be a part of the solution – you will see those in need, align your faith with your profession, and learn more about how you can bring God's goodness and protection to those who desperately need it."

Christa Hayden Sharpe, Asia Pacific Regional President,
International Justice Mission, IJM

"Patrick Talbot reminds me of my father. Like Patrick, my father was an attorney who sought to serve God through law and the culture and not just through the organized church. Although my father was a leader in the church, his influence was great outside the church as he read and thought and taught others how they should influence government, law, and culture as Christians. Thank you, Pat, for faithfully and diligently seeking to do the same and for encouraging others to follow your example."

Dr. Robert C. (Ric) Cannada, Jr., Chancellor Emeritus,
Reformed Theological Seminary

"Professor Talbot has given us a wide-ranging analysis of justice. In just 150 pages, he raises the most important issues of legal theory, as well as the real world problems relevant to those under any government setting. His experience in numerous countries and legal systems has enabled him to identify questions that will be relevant across the globe. The collections of law-related scriptures throughout the book are especially valuable. His distinction between pre-victim justice and post-victim justice in the commercial setting (p. 108) is especially helpful."

Robert F. Cochran, Jr.
Louis D. Brandeis Professor of Law, Pepperdine University School of Law
Founder and Director, Nootbaar Institute on Law, Religion, and Ethics

"I highly recommend Pat Talbot's *Improving Justice on the Earth*. With insight and clarity, the book addresses key issues that are foundational to understanding law and justice. It is deeply rooted in scripture, and it contains helpful charts that illustrate the key points. The book is ideal for both individual reading and group study. Its principled approach is desperately needed in a day where we have tremendous disagreement about things such as the proper role and structure of government, the nature of rights, and even the meaning of justice itself."

Jeffrey A. Brauch
Chairman of the Board, Advocates International
Professor, Regent University School of Law
Executive Director, Center for Global Justice, Human Rights, and the Rule of Law

IMPROVING JUSTICE ON THE EARTH

A SUMMARY CHRISTIAN WORLDVIEW ON LAW, JUSTICE AND GOVERNMENT

Study Guide

~ With Discussion Questions and Prayer Points, For Individuals and Groups ~

Patrick M. Talbot, J.D.

IMPROVING JUSTICE ON THE EARTH: A Summary Christian Worldview on Law, Justice and Government Study Guide

Published by AI ICLS, Advocates International Institute of Christian Legal Studies
Alexandria, Virginia, U.S.A.

Website: www.advocatesinternational.org

Printed August 2019

Cover Design: Yehezkiel Tanusaputra

Edited by: Kathy Talbot

ISBN: 978-0-578-55860-8

DEDICATION

To Advocates and Students Serving Jesus Christ, and
Seeking His Justice Around The World,
and
To All Who Worked With Love on this Study Guide

Righteousness And Justice Are The Foundation Of Your Throne;
Love And Faithfulness Go Before You.
(Psalm 89:14)

In faithfulness he will bring forth justice;
⁴ he will not falter or be discouraged till he establishes justice on earth.
In his teaching the islands will put their hope.
(Isaiah 42:3b-4)

Instruction will go out from me; my justice will become a light to the nations.
⁵ My righteousness draws near speedily, my salvation is on the way, and my arm will
bring justice to the nations.
(Isaiah 51:4b-5a)

TABLE OF CONTENTS

ACKNOWLEDGMENTS

TO THOSE WHO inspired, encouraged and prayed for this effort, and for us personally, I am so grateful: to Brent McBurney (supporting and inspiring this in so many ways), the founder of Advocates International, Sam Ericsson (inspiring it all); Tony and Mardiana (supporting in so many ways), David Surya (for his enthusiastic support), Frederik (especially his impressive interest, like a student's), Iman and Lia Santoso (thanks for encouraging us), and all the PPHKI intercessors; Mike Rody, Grant and Ceri, and all the LGK team (who prayed every week); JK and Sharm (keeping it moving); the Eggerts (inspiring the initial idea); Mark Mudri, Gregory Vijayendran and the AI Global Council and Board (for their encouragement throughout the years), Mike Schutt (for being a model teacher of Christian Legal Studies); to our cast of wonderful supportive students, and our many prayer and financial supporters.

I especially thank my past interns, Lily Wang (University of Ottawa) for her incredible efforts, including everything from formatting and graphics, to text and substantive links. Thanks also to Lisa Russell (Pepperdine Law) for her working with me on citations. Special appreciation must go to Hazel Tirza (Universitas Pelita Harapan) for her help with this Study Guide, in so many ways. I also am so grateful for Julia Tan and Christine Montiero for their design ideas.

Special thanks also goes to those who took time to read and offer comments and suggestions: Jeff Brauch (USA), David McIlroy (U.K.), John Eidsmoe (USA), Steve Persenaire (Indonesia), and several others, including editors.

Special thanks goes to my wife, Kathy. She initiated ideas on use of this Study Guide for small groups of students and attorneys; she contributed substantive content, and still keeps editing. She is super supportive and inspiring. I also wish to thank my loving children, Joshua, Elly, Peter, Daniel, Gloria, Katie, and Susie, whom I care so deeply for and who pray for me every day; thanks for keeping me going in prayer – some actually contributed content to this book, sharing in its value.

I especially thank my King and God, His Holy Spirit, for inspiring and guiding me in all my small, daily, and big decisions in life, and for giving me so much strength.

FOREWORD

A Book To Help You Grow!

SOME GREAT TEACHERS provide answers for their students. Others help their students ask the right questions. In his *Improving Justice on the Earth: A Summary Christian Worldview on Law, Justice and Government,* Pat Talbot does both.

Law professor, attorney, vice-president of Advocates International, Pat Talbot has been my friend for many years. As a fellow professor, I have observed his excellence in the classroom and have studied his fine scholarship. But I am especially moved by the way Pat and his wife Kathy love their students, take them under their wings, and help them grow into fine lawyers, fine citizens, and fine Christians.

The fact that some may see no need for this book is itself a reason it is necessary. Religion and law are often regarded as entirely separate realms that have nothing to do with one another. Secularists in North America and Western Europe regard law and government as their exclusive domain and resent any intrusion of religion on their territory. But their worldview assumes a paradigm that was never fully accepted in the West and never accepted at all in other parts of the world. And it is a dying paradigm, because it is intellectually bankrupt. As Professor Talbot ably demonstrates, the secular model cannot explain the origin of moral values, the source of human rights, the influence of sin, or the operation of reason itself. We cannot even begin to address these questions if our minds and hearts are closed to the possibility that God exists, that He is involved with His creation, and that his Word is relevant to questions of law and government.

But opening our minds and hearts to God and His Word does not immediately answer our questions. Rather, it provides a framework for analysis that enables us to explore the questions fully and honestly. Throughout the centuries, great Christian scholars have disagreed on the nature of justice and human rights, the relationship of love to justice and law, the proper model for civil government, the relationship of church and state, crime and punishment, economics based on the laws of God and the nature of man, and other subjects. Professor Talbot leads his readers on a voyage of exploration surveying the various schools of thought and asking probing questions that encourage the reader to think and pray about these questions and discuss them with others. And he closes with a stirring call to arms, urging his readers to devote their lives to Christian service in law and government, Improving Justice on the Earth.

Improving Justice on the Earth will answer some of your questions, but it will replace them with other, deeper questions, as Professor Talbot gently guides you on the path to developing A Summary Christian Worldview on Law, Justice and Government.

Read on!

Col. John A. Eidsmoe

Senior Counsel, Foundation for Moral Law

INTRODUCTION

IMPROVING JUSTICE ON THE EARTH AND THE IMPORTANCE OF CHRISTIAN WORLDVIEW

Instruction will go out from me; my justice will become a light to the nations. ⁵ My righteousness draws near speedily, my salvation is on the way, and my arm will bring justice to the nations. (Isaiah 51:4b-5a)

IN THIS PASSAGE in Isaiah (and in Isaiah 42:3-4), you should get a short glimpse into God's heart, specifically, His intention to establish justice on the earth, as well as in eternity. This Study Guide is designed to help you cultivate a Christian worldview – a "set of lenses" – so you can better see God's call to justice, the way He sees it. If we are to share in God's work of doing justice in the earth, we need a foundation in Scripture and history as to what that is. This is where the idea of Christian worldview comes in. It helps us build a foundation of truth for the vision and work ahead.

A *worldview* is something each of us has, even if we aren't that aware of it. It is important in helping us understand how to see the world, like a pair of glasses we wear to help us see and interpret everything in it. In short, it's our beliefs and ideas, about truth, reality, life, and how we see *everything*. If you are wearing incorrect lenses, you get a distorted view. So it is with worldviews. *Christian worldview* is about seeing life, reality, and everything in it, the way Jesus sees it.

Scripture, including careful reflection on it, along with studying ideas of solid Christian scholars in history who also sought its truth, should serve to craft the lenses we need to help us see all this in the right way. A worldview impacts everything, including our visions of law, justice, human and other rights, standards of good governance, and how all this should fit together in societies. It's important to get the right view with the right lenses. Christian worldview serves that status.

In this life of course, we can't have a completely flawless Christian worldview, because of sin; *now we see through a glass, darkly* (1 Corinthians 13:12 (KJV)), but we should do our best in seeking God for this, and Jesus assures his true disciples, "you will know the truth, and the truth will set you free." (John 8:32). It's our hope this Study Guide helps you see that truth, gaining a sure foundation of ideas so you can best share in Christ's work of establishing justice on the earth.

I have attempted in this Study Guide to summarize some of the strongest components of Christian worldview on law, justice, and government, as I see it (some subjects, including some International ones, I have saved for a subsequent Student Handbook). This Study Guide should give you several insights on improving justice and legal systems in your own countries. Importantly, this also helps us fulfill the Great Commission of going and making disciples of all nations (Matthew 28:18-20), In turn, this serves the Greatest Commands in Scripture, to love God with all we are, and our neighbors as ourselves (Mark 12:30-31; Luke 10:27); how better to do that than by helping our neighbors experience justice?

This Study Guide, provides information on these subjects:

- in Part I (Chapters 1-4): the significance of Creation for shaping law and justice, a biblical view of human rights, how law and justice help fulfill the command to love our neighbors, and a summary of secular and Scriptural schools of law (jurisprudence);
- in Part II (Chapters 5-11): optimal shapes of social structures that advance justice, a study of the best kinds of government and economic systems known in history, and a study on Law and Economic Development culminating and tying together many of the concepts in this booklet;

- in Part III (Chapter 12): here we consider your career and calling to serve Jesus Christ, introducing you more fully to Advocates International.

Six Appendices, five external links to supplemental aids (diagrams, tables, videos, and charts), and several weblinks in text and footnotes to outside sources, should serve you in gaining more information and a greater understanding of the ideas in this study.

This Study Guide is part of a series of resources being developed by Advocates International (AI) as part of its Resource Center, and its Institute of Christian Legal Studies (AI ICLS). Great new resources are available at the Resources and Institute page of AI's website, which is constantly being updated: http://resources.advocatesinternational.org/.

I hope this short Study Guide enables you to serve Jesus better, *to do justice with compassion,* in your careers and callings.

P. Talbot

Vice President AI, Director AI ICLS

HOW TO USE THIS GUIDE

Do not conform to the pattern of this world but be transformed by the renewing of your mind. (Romans 12:2)

As iron sharpens iron, so one man sharpens another. (Proverbs 27:17)

Individual and Group Study Tips

WHILE YOU CAN benefit by using this Study Guide individually, we encourage you to gather together with other lawyers, law students or advocates to look at what the Bible and historical experiences say about law, justice and government.

1. We encourage you to meet weekly or monthly with your local advocates or student group, or to start a group with several lawyers, law students, or legal professionals for this study.
2. Read the chapter and meditate on the Scriptures individually before meeting together. Think and write your answers to the questions, then pray before discussing these.
3. Meet with your group and discuss the materials, and the questions and answers.
4. Pray with your group and commit to accountability.
5. Decide on an advocacy project that you can start working on together (see Chapter 12).

Supplemental Aids (Please make ample use of these, including):

1. *Links in Footnotes to Videos and Websites.* Several videos and supporting articles are included in text and footnotes, especially in Chapter 1 on Creation, and in Chapter 9, an important one on various kinds of

government. These short, dynamic informative and sometimes entertaining videos give you a whole course.

2. *Six Informative Appendices.* Several (I, V, VI) are lists of Scriptures covering the subjects of justice, good government, bribery and injustice. Study these Scripture lists often. The other Appendices include annotated charts, tables, and diagrams supplementing information in the chapters. Appendix VII is a list of additional study aids available on AI's website, connecting you to some outside materials from this author.

3. *Additional Study Aids (Appendix VII).* These items are mentioned throughout the text, and compiled in Appendix VII. They include some diagrams, slides and short essays on important topics, such as separation of Church and State, corruption and poverty, and what it is like to be a Christian lawyer. A link to these materials is available on our website, this page: https://resources.advocatesinternational.org/ai-resources

PART I

ON LAW, JUSTICE AND RIGHTS

CHAPTER 1

CREATION: ITS SIGNIFICANCE FOR LAW AND JUSTICE

In the beginning God created the heavens and the earth.
(Genesis 1:1, NIV)[1]

So What Is the Significance? Suppose for a moment there is no God, no Creator. What impact would that have on our understanding of law and justice? Well, if there were no God, how can anyone know the difference between right and wrong, or good and evil, or just and unjust conduct? Such things would only be a matter of individual preference or opinion, or a prevailing consensus, all of which can change at any time. In contrast, if there is a Creator God, it would make all the difference in the world in helping us see real standards of right and wrong, and in helping us define good and evil, justice and injustice. That is because such things would be based on the objective standards of an Ultimate Authority (God), and not on merely subjective human viewpoints.

Everyone knows law should be based on good, moral and just standards, not on what is immoral and unjust, and this is so we, as humans, can know what it means to act rightly. But, if there is not a Creator God, we cannot be sure of *what is*

---

[1] All references in this Study Guide to Scripture, unless otherwise indicated, are from *The Holy Bible, New International Version* (Zondervan 1984, 2011); *The Holy Bible, New International Version* (Biblica 2011), *available at* https://www.biblegateway.com/versions/ New-International-Version-NIV-Bible/#booklist.

right and just, or if anything like that even exists. We can shape our human laws according to standards of what is right and just only if there is a God, and only if He can show us what these standards are. For Christians, this idea is not hard to grasp. Regrettably, however, our secular colleagues don't think as we do. So, it is important to know there is a God who has established real standards of what is right and just, and to even defend these principles to our secular and atheistic colleagues.

This short chapter aims to help you do that. Fortunately, recent scientific discoveries in something known as Intelligent Design (ID), help us clearly see, through science, that a Creator God most certainly exists.[2]

Intelligent Design. ID is usually discussed at two levels: (i) the intricate design of life, including even in a single cell, and (ii) the clear evidences of design in the cosmos (the universe). I shall just touch on some quick examples of each aspect.

Consider this example of ID in the tiny living, *bacterial flagellum* (Fig. 1.1):[3]

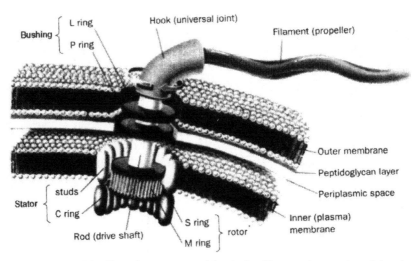

Fig 1.1 The bacterial flagellum, showing gears and functioning like an engine on a boat. It is a favorite example showing the intricate design of its Creator God.

---

[2] Scriptures such as *Romans* 1:19-20 and *Psalm* 19 show that God has already made Himself known to everyone through His Creation.

[3] See image in, J. Warner Wallace, *Is God Real? The Bacterial Flagellum and the Divine Design Inference*, (Apr. 17, 2014), http://coldcasechristianity.com/2014/is-god-real-the-bacterial-flagellum-and-the-divine-design-inference/ (internal citations omitted).

All the known pieces of this tiny *flagellum* must be in place at the same time for it to ever function. This means it is improbable it could have evolved, with different parts emerging at different times. Its functioning requires the existence of all its parts at precisely the same time. It is *irreducibly complex*, having all its necessary pieces simultaneously in place, all according to its architect's blueprints.

In this table, Dr. Stephen Meyer shows the probability of amino acids forming into just the right proteins to create something alive is about zero (1 chance in 10^{164}).[4] Compare the chance of that happening to other calculations in this table.

Chances of finding a functional protein by chance $= 1/10^{164}$
10^{80} elementary particles in the universe
10^{16} seconds since the Big Bang
10^{139} events since the beginning of the universe

As Dr. Meyer notes, there are fewer seconds in time since the dawn of the universe than the chance of amino acids accidentally forming into useful proteins. He concludes, no serious scientist today still thinks life happened by chance.[5]

On a cosmic scale, the entire universe is fine tuned for life. Again, this points to the ID of its Creator God.[6] The probability of the universe having the initial low entropy (decay) it needed to sustain itself, and of this happening by sheer chance, is $1:10^{10(123)}$ (almost impossibly small).[7]

---

[4] The Bible Smith, *Amino Acid Sequencing, No serious scientist thinks that life began by chance,* YouTube (Aug. 26, 2015), https://www.youtube.com/watch?v=NoH68HhS2HQ (from Stephen D. Meyer, Video Lecture, Does God Exist? True U (Focus on the Family) (2012)).

[5] *Id.*

[6] William Lane Craig, *The Fine-Tuning of the Universe,* YouTube (June 8, 2016), https://www.youtube.com/watch?v=EE76nwimuT0; *See also* The John Ankerberg Show, *How does the fine tuning of the universe point to an intelligent designer?,* YouTube (Nov. 11, 2017), https://www.youtube.com/watch?v=I37dj9cbgUE.

[7] *ID's Top Six – The Fine-Tuning of the Universe,* Evolution News & Science Today (Nov. 8, 2017), https://evolutionnews.org/2017/11/ids-top-six-the-fine-tuning-of-the-universe/.

How Does This Information Apply to Issues of Law and Justice? Scripture indicates we are created in the image of God (Genesis 1:27), so we should be able to grasp true moral knowledge, implanted in us by God (called *Natural Law* (NL), see Romans 1:19; 2:14-15 in support). We can (and do) use this knowledge to fashion good laws that promote justice.[8] In this way, we should strive to conduct our lives according to God's good standards. Some of these standards will informally regulate our day-to-day interactions; others will more formally be incorporated into actual laws. Yet because humans have sinful natures (we are fallen), we tend to redefine good and evil contrary to God's standards (Genesis 3:5), and this is something we should vigilantly guard against. Secular atheists, however, don't think this way.

So What Are the Problems for Those Who Reject a Creator God? Atheistic evolutionists believe in something called *Scientific Materialism*, and hold the universe and life came from nothing. They say there is no God to cause anything, and so they have no real basis for knowing if some action is truly right or wrong (again it's just a matter of human opinion). But atheists often contradict themselves, claiming *there are* such things as objective right and wrong, justice and injustice (i.e., moral truth). They simply lack a solid basis to assert their claim, since they have no higher standards (apart from only human ones), by which to evaluate their own subjective, human standards.

C.S. Lewis explains the problem this way:

Suppos[e] there was no intelligence behind the universe, no creative mind. In that case, nobody designed my brain for the purpose of thinking. It is merely that when the atoms inside my skull happen, for physical or chemical reasons, to arrange themselves in a certain way, this gives me, as a by-product, the sensation I call thought. But, if so, how can I trust my own thinking to be true? It's like upsetting a milk jug and hoping that the way it splashes itself will give you a map of London. But if I can't trust my own thinking, of course I can't trust the arguments

---

[8] Just how we come to know these standards is the subject of other chapters in Part I.

leading to Atheism, and therefore have no reason to be an Atheist, or anything else. **Unless I believe in God, I cannot believe in thought**: so I can never use thought to disbelieve in God.[9] (emphasis added).

The secular atheists' insistence on *any* absolute standards of moral right and wrong only suggests an Ultimate Authority on the matter (God).

A second problem stems from secular atheists' rejection of the idea of sin. Consequently, they are more likely to err in their moral judgments, and sin against God's standards, since they don't even believe He exists. This doesn't mean Christians are always accurate in their moral judgments; after all, Christians also have a sinful nature and are capable of getting it wrong, but at least they know there are correct standards to live by, as set-forth by God. Nor does this mean secular atheists are incapable of making sound moral judgments and passing just laws; after all, secular atheists are created in God's image, even if they will not admit it and choose to reject God as the source of their moral wisdom.

In Sum: ID Science's Impact on Law. Since ID scientifically shows a very high probability there is a Creator God, we can be certain there are objective standards of good and evil by which humans should govern themselves.[10] These come from a Higher Authority (God), and are not subject to shifting human views. We should be able to use this moral information to fashion good laws and benefit our societies. As students, this should be one of your chief aims in law. Atheists can't see this. They can, however, also help make good laws, and occasionally render good moral judgments, because God has imparted into them His basic moral knowledge (NL), and given them consciences, although they deny His existence.

Standards of Evidence and Burdens of Proof. Some information is needed here as to what it means to establish a case. If the issue of whether a Creator God exists were submitted as a case in court, the burden should be on secular atheists to prove God does not exist, (i.e., not the other way around, for Creationists or

---

[9] C.S. Lewis, The Case for Christianity 32 (1942).

[10] There are Young Earth and Old Earth Creationists. Their ongoing debate in no way alters the conclusion law can have true moral content, because of the existence of a Creator God.

ID supporters to prove God does exist, since the secularist seeks to change the status quo of human thought). Since the evidence (statistics above, etc.) shows an extremely low probability the secularists' scenario is true, *they cannot prove their case*.

In most legal scenarios, a case can be proven by 51% of the evidence supporting one side's case (as in civil suits; i.e., this is called the *greater weight*, or a *preponderance* of the evidence). In some serious cases, proof is established by about 70-75% of the evidence (i.e., *clear and convincing evidence*). In criminal cases, proof of guilt is only established by about 95% of the evidence (i.e., *beyond a reasonable doubt*).[11] Secularists cannot establish their case against God, even under the more lenient, *greater weight* (51%) of the evidence, standard.

If for any reason, however, the burden of proof should shift to Creationists or ID supporters to support a case for God, the voluminous data in favor of ID and Creation has already established His existence by greater that 51% of the evidence, and possibly beyond a reasonable doubt.[12] The case is over, and favors a Creator.

Identifying the Creator. So who is this Creator God, and Intelligent Designer of it all? Of course, He is the God revealed in the Bible (Genesis through Revelation), as Jesus Christ himself attested, and who also rightly claimed to be God (see Colossians 1:15-16). Jesus' testimony is validated by his own resurrection from the dead (a historically verifiable event, never repeated in history by any other religious leader).[13]

---

[11] *Standards of Proof*, CAMPUSCLARITY BLOG (Oct. 15, 2013), https://home.campusclarity.com/standards-of-proof/.

[12] See text, including statistics, and notes above (*supra*, notes 3-7, 9).

[13] GARY HABERMAS, The Resurrection Evidence that Changed Current Scholarship, YOUTUBE, Biola University, September 14, 2013, https://www.youtube.com/watch?v=5znVUFHqO4Q.

DISCUSSION QUESTIONS:

1. Why is it important for human lawmakers to know there is a Creator God in today's relativistic world?

2. Can morality be contextualized into different situations if there is a Creator who is absolute? If so, how? (Hint: this is not discussed in this chapter, and will come up again later, but you should give it some thought now.)

3. What evidences do you see for ID in the cosmos and in living things, beyond the examples in this short chapter? Why do you think it may be difficult for some people to see ID? (Hint: consider the Romans 1 and 2 passages in the text above.)

4. How does knowing there are objective moral standards help you understand the role of law in society? How does this knowledge influence your own Christian walk?

PRAYER POINTS:

1. Pray that as you acknowledge God as Creator of the universe, that you would walk closer with Him, and that you can influence others in the truth.
2. Knowing that you are made in the image of God, pray that your daily actions would reflect God's glory in your legal or similar career.
3. Pray for your leaders in government to make and enforce laws that are good and just, acknowledging the standards of their Creator.

CHAPTER 2

JUSTICE AND RIGHTS

Righteousness and justice are the foundation of [God's] throne.
(Psalm 89:14)

He has shown you, O mortal, what is good. And what does the Lord require
of you? To act justly and to love mercy and to walk humbly with your God.
(Micah 6:8)

~God wants us to be Maximalists in doing Justice, not Minimalists, to go
beyond our legal duties, and meet someone's actual needs.~

BECAUSE WE KNOW there is a Creator God, we also know there are such things
as moral right and wrong, justice and injustice, good and evil (i.e., ethics).
Accordingly, we have available to us this substance called *justice* to guide our human conduct, including by making good laws. But how can we know what is just
and right, or unjust? What is this substance called *justice*?

A. JUSTICE

Scriptural Foundation
Since God's character is just, and we are to live and act justly, Scripture should
be our starting point in studying *justice*. Here are some basic Scriptures on justice,
as it concerns God and humans (a more comprehensive list is in Appendix I)[14]:

---

[14] I have bolded both the words ***justice*** and ***righteousness*** (and their derivatives) in these
passages, since their meaning is essentially the same.

1 Kings 10:9. *[H]e has made you king to maintain **justice** and **righteousness**.*

Psalm 9:8. *He rules the world in **righteousness** and **judges** the peoples with equity.*

Psalm 11:7. *For the LORD is **righteous**, he loves **justice**; the **upright** will see his face.*

Psalm 89:14. ***Righteousness** and **justice** are the foundation of your throne.*

Psalm 97:2. ***[R]ighteousness** and **justice** are the foundation of his throne.*

Psalm 103:6. *The LORD works **righteousness** and **justice** for all the oppressed.*

Psalm 106:3. *Blessed are those who act **justly**, who always do what is **right**.*

Proverbs 21:15. *When **justice** is done, it brings joy to the **righteous** but terror to evildoers.*

Isaiah 9:7. *He will reign on David's throne and over his kingdom, establishing and upholding it with **justice** and **righteousness** from that time on and forever. The zeal of the LORD Almighty will accomplish this.*

Isaiah 28:17. *I will make **justice** the measuring line and **righteousness** the plumb line . . . .*

Isaiah 42:4. *[H]e will not falter or be discouraged till he establishes **justice** on earth.*

Isaiah 56:1. *This is what the LORD says: "Maintain **justice** and do what is **right** . . . . "*

Hosea 12:6. *[M]aintain love and **justice**, and wait for your God always.*

Amos 5:24. *But let **justice** roll on like a river, **righteousness** like a never-failing stream!*

Micah 6:8b. *And what does the Lord require of you? To act **justly**, and to love mercy, and to walk humbly with your God.*

Zephaniah 3:5. *Morning by morning he dispenses his **justice** . . . .*

Zechariah 7:9. *This is what the LORD Almighty said: "Administer true **justice**; show mercy and compassion to one another."*

Matthew 12:18. *I will put my Spirit on him, and he will proclaim **justice** to the nations.*

Matthew 12:20. *A bruised reed he will not break, and a smoldering wick he will not snuff out, till he has brought **justice** through to victory.*

Matthew 23:23. *But you have neglected the more important matters of the law—**justice**, mercy and faithfulness. You should have practiced the latter, without neglecting the former.*

Luke 18:8. *I tell you, he will see that they get **justice**, and quickly.*

Scripture, in the Old Testament (OT), defines justice very broadly, and actually synonymously with righteousness. It uses two Hebrew words for this: *tzedakah* (or *tzedek*-slightly more *societal*), meaning righteousness/justice more in the everyday affairs of people; and *mishpat*, dealing with justice in a more formal judicial, or civil government sense.[15] But they essentially mean the same thing. In the New Testament (NT), the Greek word, *diakonia* is used, and also has the shared meaning of justice and righteousness.[16]

Additional Definitions (Positive and Negative Sides to Justice)

Aristotle, in ancient Greece, had a similarly broad idea of justice, as a virtue, or as *Virtue*, in character.[17] Some people define justice as *rights*, as in giving people their rights or enforcing their rights, as in something they should *get*, as *due* them (see more on this below).[18] I think this is true in part, but I agree with the broader definitions of justice above, like virtue and righteousness. St. Augustine added a definition of justice which I have found very useful (especially when coupled with the broader OT ideas above). His idea of justice is *giving to each his due*,[19] (simi-

---

[15] *See* Timothy Keller, *What Is Biblical Justice? Tim Keller On One Of The Bible's Most Misunderstood Ideas*, RELEVANT (Aug. 23, 2012), http://www.relevantmagazine.com/god/practical-faith/what-biblical-justice.

[16] Compare the NIV and KJV of *Romans* 1:17 in English; what do you see in the translations?

[17] *See Justice As A Virtue*, STANFORD ENCYCLOPEDIA OF PHILOSOPHY, (Jan. 21, 2016), https://plato.stanford.edu/entries/justice-virtue/ (contrasting Plato and Aristotle).

[18] Nicholas J. Wolterstorff, *Response to My Commentators* (2010), www.klice.co.uk/uploads/SCEWolterstorff%20extended%20version.doc (last visited July 28, 2018).

[19] Mary T. Clark, *Augustine on Justice, available at* http://www.patristique.org/sites/patristique.org/IMG/pdf/63_ix_1_2_05.pdf (last visited Aug. 1, 2018). Henri di Bracton (d. 1268), a Christian jurist, similarly said that justice was the "constant . . . will to award to each his right." HENRI DI BRACTON, ON THE LAWS AND CUSTOMS OF ENGLAND, 2 Bracton Online 23, *available at* http://bracton.law.harvard.edu/Unframed/English/v2/23.htm (last visited July 30, 2018). John Rawls, more recently, offered that justice is essentially *fairness*, which isn't necessarily wrong, but he doesn't really define *fairness* as something objective (say from Scripture). He only suggests it is a consensus arrived at by a group of like-minded people (stripped of ideologies and things like Christianity), who think like him. *See* Tsun-En Lu, *John Rawls's 'Justice as Fairness' and the Pluralistic Society: A Christian Critique*

lar to Aristotle). That basically means giving each what they *deserve* (in English we sometimes refer to this as one's *just desserts*). However, take note that not everything *due* someone is a *right* (as in something good or **Positive**, a benefit, s/he should have). It is certainly often a **Negative**, as in a consequence, or a punishment, for something improper s/he has done. This is perhaps the most common understanding of justice known in society, but it still is a *good* thing.[20]

Notice also Augustine would concur with the idea of giving or vindicating one's *rights* (something *positive* that is *due* them), as an expression of justice, above. That is, if someone has a *right* to something, it is *due* them, and for every right there is usually a corresponding *duty* (an *obligation due*) on someone's part to fulfill it. This idea of corresponding rights and duties also reflects a lot of what we commonly think of as justice. And yet, the broader ideas of justice (above), as righteousness and virtue, include this meaning yet surpass it. I consider this broader, second view to be more accurate.[21]

The idea of giving people what is due them is too often interpreted only in a **negative** sense, such as punishment for a crime. For example, if someone steals money from his company, gets caught, and goes to jail, we might say, "he got what he deserved," or "justice was served." If he pays back what he owes the company, we might also happily say justice has now been done for the victim (this payment relates to a kind of justice, called *restorative justice*, explained in my longer Handbook).[22] That's well and good. Justice certainly contemplates this punitive meaning against the thief, but that is not all it includes. Justice also

---

(Mar. 13, 2012),http://tsunenlu.net/2012/03/13/john-rawlss-justice-as-fairness-and-the-pluralistic-society-a-christian-critique/ (last visited Mar. 31, 2016) (analyzing Rawls's *Theory of Justice* (1973)).

[20] It should not to be confused with something *bad*, despite the word, *negative*, used to describe it.

[21] Some acts of virtue, like keeping good care of your property and body (brushing your teeth, etc.) are not based on someone else's rights, but are still just and virtuous acts.

[22] Scholars have sought to categorize justice into specific kinds; e.g., from Aristotle: *Restorative (Corrective;* rectifying wrongs), *Distributive* (a fair share of goods), *Retributive* (punishments), and *Procedural* justice (due process). Christian scholars, throughout history, have kept or sometimes changed these categories (i.e., Grotius). See Appendix II (short table summarizing such kinds).

includes a ***positive***, *giving* side, as in giving someone a benefit or reward that is *due* them (i.e., giving it to one who is *deserving*). So, if you, as a student, have successfully completed all your courses with passing grades, along with all the other requirements, you are entitled to graduate with a degree and receive your diploma. It is a right *due* you; it is *just* and *right* that you should receive it. If the university withholds your diploma, that would be *unjust*.

This conferring of a degree and diploma is a *positive* expression of justice (i.e., a *right*, indicated above); the example of the criminal verdict against the stealing employee is a *negative* one. I mean by this a punishment or consequence is received for a wrongful act, in contrast to a benefit, or reward earned or due.[23] In the world of justice, *rights* can be fulfilled (Positive side), and *punishments* can be administered (Negative side).

The idea of justice as something *due* also conjures the idea of an *amount* or *quantity* of something necessary to satisfy it, such as a payment for shoes one buys, or a fine, or an amount of jail time for a crime, and perhaps a piece of bread for a hungry child (an idea of *biblical social justice*). This is important for distinguishing justice from other actions, in which something *is not* due (as in some *gratuitous acts of kindness*; see below).

B. RIGHTS, ESPECIALLY HUMAN RIGHTS

Basic Kinds

In regard to honoring rights, as a subset of justice, it helps to note that not all rights are *human rights* (these are but a subset of all rights we can honor). In a contract for instance, if I promise to sell you white tennis shoes and you agree to pay $100 for them, I have a right to the price, and you have the right to the

---

[23] This should not be confused with positive (+) or negative (-) verbal expressions of the same acts. E.g., giving a student her diploma (+) is the same as not withholding it (-), but the overall quality of the act is positive, as in giving or conferring a benefit, not negative, as in a punishment. In the case of the criminal employee, similarly, sending him to jail (+) (an affirmative act), is the same as withholding his freedoms (-), but the overall quality of the act is negative, as in imposing a consequence for his wronging. We should be concerned more with this overall characterization of the just act (Positive vs. Negative), than with the linguistic style (+) or (-), used in expressing it.

shoes, and each of has a duty: I, to deliver the shoes, and you to pay me money. These are *legal*, contract rights. In a tort case, if I fall on a sidewalk because of your negligence in keeping it safe, I have a right to damages for my sprained ankle, and you have a duty to pay it. But these examples are not the same as *human rights* (rights we have just for being humans, and as coming from being created in God's image).[24]

Some rights are human rights, some are only *legal rights* (like the contract payment), and some are *civil rights* (which may not always reflect human rights, and in some cases are vulgar distortions of virtue and improperly called rights, but are issued as protections by the State anyway). Some rights can be in more than one category, or in all three: the *right to life* is a *human right*, a *civil right* (in most States), and a *legal right*. The right to vote is only a *civil* or *legal right* (it is not inherent in humanity, but a right to have one's say to his government could be). See Appendix III.

Problems with Rights
Some problems have emerged in the area of human rights. For instance: (1) If we have these rights because God created us in His image, with true value given us, atheists will have a hard time justifying human rights. Recall they have no clear objective moral standard for rights. (2) The list of human rights keeps expanding beyond true limits. People are becoming very individualistic and starting to claim all their individual *wants* as human rights (needs). But, all rights, including human rights (as a kind of *thing* one has), must be grounded on that which is Right (capital "R" as something good, or righteous); that is, they must be just.[25]

---

[24] A right to compensation for wrongs done against someone, in general, is arguably included as a human right. The important thing in human rights, however, is we are talking about rights you have simply by being human, before any violation of them, or any incident occurs; such as, life, liberty, speech, assembly, conscience, bodily safety.

[25] *See* THOMAS K. JOHNSON, HUMAN RIGHTS, A CHRISTIAN PRIMER 82-84 (2008), *available at* https://www.vomcanada.com/download/human_rights_johnson.pdf; *see* Oliver O'Donovan and Joan L. O'Donovan, *Hugo Grotius (1583-1646), in* FROM IRENAEUS TO GROTIUS: A SOURCEBOOK IN CHRISTIAN POLITICAL THOUGHT 787-92 (Oliver O'Donovan and Joan L. O'Donovan eds.,1999) (explaining Right vs. right in the context of Hugo Grotius' views on justice).

In this sense, "*Right*," has an *objective* meaning, and is like an *adjective*, describing the just quality of something (a law, or conduct can be Right); whereas, "right," has a *subjective* meaning, as in something one can own or possess, (e.g., one can have a right to live, eat, or vote), and so is used as a *noun*. Such terminology and distinctions should be useful in studying sections ahead.

So for instance, I do not have a right to marry someone of the same sex, even if I wanted to (I don't), and even if the State calls it a "civil right," because it is not Right (just). The same can be said for the so-called "right" to abort one's child. It is not a right because it is not Right, in almost all situations.

A good working list of real human rights, gleaned from some Christian scholars, is located in Appendix III.

C. PUTTING IT TOGETHER:
JUSTICE AND RIGHTS IN ACTIONS

It would be good at this point to pause and consider how justice and rights come together in conduct (actions) we engage in as humans every day. Imagine first a ***bottom line*** that separates justice from injustice. Below that line are acts of injustice (these should not be tolerated). Above the line are three strata of human action that should be considered *just*. The first stratum, immediately above the line are acts of justice done simply as adherence to the law, in formal legal systems. The second (and higher) stratum above the bottom line is justice done above and beyond the law. The story of the Good Samaritan (G S) in Luke 10: 27-37 is a classic illustration of this stratum. Other illustrations could include feeding the hungry, caring for the sick and needy (including building hospitals), educating those lacking access to education, and so on. The third (and highest) stratum above the line is probably best described not as justice at all, but simply as love. Loving and gracious acts of kindness done at this level likely go beyond the call of justice, as they don't seek to rectify any actual injustices, or address any true human needs or lacks.

Some specifics on these three strata (levels) is next. A table/diagram (Table 2.1) showing each of these strata, visually stacking them above the bottom line of injustice and summarizing their features into certain categories, is located at the end this chapter, for some more careful study.[26] (Small diagrams in the margins below correspond with the strata in Table 2.1 at the end of this chapter.)

1. Justice In/Through Law (lowest stratum). People act rightly and with justice toward one another here because the State civil law, or similar legal authority, requires it.[27] The State civil law expressly protects certain rights (Human Rights, Civil Rights, and other Various Private, Transactional Legal Rights), and it

Love, Not Justice
Justice Above Law
Justice In Law   (Duties + Rights;   State Enforcing; Minimalist)
INJUSTICE

imposes duties on others to satisfy those rights. Rights and duties **correspond** to each other as spelled-out in the State legal system. Just actions done in this stratum reflect what might be called a **minimalist** stance on justice, because people are acting justly in satisfaction of their legal duties, but are not yet going above and beyond such legal obligations.[28] Justice here is secured in and through a legal system.

Both the Positive (providing) and Negative (punitive) sides of justice are at work in the State's legal system.[29] Actors providing its justice may come from either the private sector, or of course, the State itself (in either its positive

---

[26] Studying Table 2.1 should help you with ideas and terms in the next few chapters. An annotated version of this table, with explanations, and illustrations, is available through a link in Appendix VII (it's for the stout in heart and mind, who really want to know more).

[27] This is not to suggest people aren't *happy* to do their duties, but such are legally enforceable, and violations (breaches) shall have consequences; *see infra*, n. 28. The word *State* in this context means any civil (public) governing authority, whether national or local. The principles here, however, apply as well to similarly situated legal authorities in many non-State institutions in society. Such social institutions (spheres) typically have some kind of formal rules and internal legal systems (governance) of their own, including structures like bylaws, codes of conduct, and SOPs. Examples include hospitals, churches, families, schools, corporations, and NGOs. The three strata of actions discussed above apply in these non-State social institutions as well. See Chapter 7, discussing these.

[28] In no way is this intended to imply actors in this stratum never fulfill their duties with a sense of compassion (consider a State social worker having to remove a child from a sexually abusive parent, or someone paying a personal injury award with a sense of compassion for the victim, etc.).

[29] As is true also in non-State social institutions (school's, families, corporations), where similar, formal rule-making authority exists.

(providing), or negative (enforcing) capacities).[30] Lastly, a quantum or some amount is due to satisfy justice (i.e., enforcing a right, imposing a prison term, a fine, an amount of compensation for injury, specific performance, etc.)

2. Justice Above Law (a higher stratum). Here, someone (i.e., a Good Samaritan) acts rightly towards another voluntarily, out of a sense of compassion, but not from a legal duty. A real right (usually a human or civil right) such as life, safety, or property is at stake. It is threatened or already deprived. State civil law does not impose any duty upon the volunteer to act. His

Love, Not Justice
Justice Above Law **(Rectifying, Just Mercies)** (About Rights, Not Legal Duties; Non-State; Maximalist)
Justice In Law
INJUSTICE

actions may come out of a sense of **moral obligation** and **conscience**, or as a **calling** from God. Such voluntary acts of mercy should still be seen as acts of justice since they satisfy or restore (repair) actual injury to someone's rights.[31] In the story of the Good Samaritan, the Samaritan attended to the basic human rights and needs of the victim of a vicious robbery and attack, but he did so without any State law requiring it.[32]

This reflects what might be called a **maximalist** stance on justice because it surpasses the actor's duties under law. In this stratum, we should see a real right

---

[30] Some thinkers incorrectly assume justice is something exclusively in the realm of the State. Yet even in the areas discussed above, where the State has enforcement authority, justice is often satisfied by private parties (i.e., paying a bill, tendering goods or lands sold, a store owner respecting someone's civil rights, etc.) Also, as said before (*supra* n. 27), other social institutions (churches, businesses, etc.) can implement justice through their formal rule-making authority.

[31] Some incorrectly say this reflects Love or Mercy, not Justice. It actually is both.

[32] States in recent times have attempted to impose a legal duty on bystanders to render aid to victims (e.g., some Scandinavian ones). This is different than the Levite and priest who passed by the victim in the Good Samaritan story. Jesus emphasized they may have broken God's moral law to love their neighbor by not helping, but they did not go to jail under State law for illegal conduct (the thieves who beat the man do deserve that). How do you feel about the State imposing such duties of aid? What if the aid is not immediate assistance, but something like building a hospital, or school, or providing clean water to an impoverished community in your country: should the government impose a law to compel private citizens to do that (can it compel, *volunteerism*, or "*social justice*")?

is at stake, but absent is a corresponding duty in law clearly imposed on someone else to satisfy it.

The Negative (punitive) side of justice is not involved. A quantum of something to restore justice or a deprived right, however, is. In the G S story, this includes the amount of time, money and effort invested to bandage the victim's wounds, get him to an inn, and pay the innkeeper to see to his cure, and all as voluntary.

Actors in this stratum are usually not the State, but private individuals or groups (NGOs).[33] Some would call the G S story and similar acts, examples of **social justice** (notice in the G S story justice was done for someone without State involvement). It is likely better to call this ***biblical justice*** (or at least ***biblical social justice***). Sadly, social justice today is very often being redefined as a secular Statist activity, giving people their *wants* (not *needs*) or even things that are *improper* to give them in the first place. [34]

Something is not a true right, however, if it is not also Right (isn't virtuous). Students should avoid secular ideas of social justice, so common today, which seek to vindicate false rights. In the Church, too many are indiscriminately adopting *social justice* as part of its vocabulary, without careful considering its meaning.

3. Love, Not Justice (highest stratum). Here, we see people acting toward others above and beyond the scope of justice, in loving acts of kindness, which don't actually respond to any real need, or threat, or deprivation of someone's rights. This is more akin to love than justice. Similar to the intermediate stratum (G S)

Love, Not Justice (Loving Kindness) (Not about Rights or Duties; Non-State; Maximalist)
Justice Above Law
Justice In Law
INJUSTICE

---

[33] A State *can* be involved in some instances in providing this. Consider its discretionary use of aid to help victims of some natural disaster in a foreign land, and similar examples.

[34] Examples include making sure everyone has the same income or goods in society, instead of (biblically) an equal opportunity to advance their lives and callings in accordance with their abilities. The first situation too often requires taking things from some people and giving them to others who didn't earn it – a simple prelude to Communism (see later chapters). Some also incorrectly claim shifting sexual identities and same-sex marriage as "rights" of social justice.

actors are not acting out of a civil law obligation, yet unlike that stratum, they are not responding to any injustice, suffering, or true deprivation of human rights, either (there is no real need to address). In this stratum there is neither a real right at stake, nor a corresponding duty to act. Showing affection, sending a greeting card to a friend, or doing something nice for another (watering the neighbor's plants, without being asked or without any reciprocal arrangement to do so).

Some suggest, perhaps validly, this sort of conduct still fits within the scope of justice, in its broadest meaning as righteousness and virtue (discussed above). Support for this may also be found in Romans 13:7, indicating Christians have a continuing *debt* to love others, suggesting something is *due* or *deserved* (isn't that a key feature of justice?).[35] The difficulty in this suggestion, however, is determining the amount or quantity of any kindness actually *due* or measurable to satisfy some injustice or repair someone's human lack, or a deprivation of rights. This feature of justice is missing (after all, how much sharing of your ice cream do I really *need*?). I suggest acts in this stratum, while certainly not unjust, exceed and are distinct from the regular meaning of justice.

If, however, we are to view these acts as sorts of justice, this of course reflects a **maximalist** stance (as no civil law duties were invoked). The Negative side of justice is also not involved. Actors, again, are typically not the State, but private sector parties (some exceptions, I suppose, can be imagined).

Conclusion. As Jesus' followers, we should strive to be **maximalists**, not **minimalists** in doing justice, as the Good Samaritan story shows us. As Christian *lawyers*, we also have another step to take. *Our job is to make sure justice in our legal systems (Section A in Table 2.1) comports with God's standards of what is Right and just.*

---

[35] This interpretation would seem to incorrectly convert all acts of compassion into justice, essentially erasing any meaningful distinction between love and justice.

DISCUSSION QUESTIONS:

1. Are there situations in our society currently in which we are given some sort of right by the State, but that would not be a Right biblically? In those circumstances, how ought we to respond as Christians? As Christian lawyers?

2. How do the different expressions of justice listed above reflect Christian standards? How can we be maximalists in everyday justice?

3. Is your legal system just or unjust? Support your answer with examples.

4. How does knowing that there is an Intelligent Designer (a Creator God), from Chapter 1, tie in with the idea of set standards for justice and law? Is it possible for human lawmakers to violate these standards, and if so, can you think of any examples where you see this happening?

PRAYER POINTS:

1. Pray that you would know and understand how to "do justice, love mercy and walk humbly with your God." (Micah 6:8)
2. Pray that you would live righteously and encourage those around you, in love, to do the same.
3. Pray for your current leadership in your country to act with justice, including religious leaders, attorneys, judges, lawmakers, business people and government employees.

SPECIAL APPENDIX TO CH. 2 (Table 2.1): A Taxonomy Of Justice And Rights By Actions
(See fully annotated version with explanations available in Appendix VII) © 2018 P Talbot

SECTIONS A, B, C (Category & Description of Actions, Rights, and Justice Involved)	Are There Corresponding Rights & Duties? (Y/N)	Is it Related to Justice? (Minimalist v. Maximalist)	Actions and Actors (State v. Private)		Quantifiable (Amount of Something Due)
			Positive, Providing Side of Justice = (Giving Benefits, Rewards Due, Satisfying Rights, Caring for Needs)	Negative, Punitive Side of Justice = (Imposing Sanctions, Consequences on Wrongdoing, Correcting, Rectifying)	
Matching Location in Diagram 3.1, Love, Just, Law:			*(Actions or Inactions Can Effectuate Either Kind)*		
LOVE, NOT JUSTICE (LOVING KINDNESS) High Arc **C** Love to Love Acts of Kindness not due or expected; not meeting a clear need, lack, or right; *no need, no aid.*	Right: No Duty: No	**Likely Not Justice.** If Justice, in its broadest biblical sense as virtue (see Rom 13:8), it is *Maximalist*	Inapplicable (nothing due) **Actors: Private: Yes State: No** **Examples:** signs of friendship, sharing an ice cream, sending a greeting card; doing something nice for s.o. without being asked or required.	Inapplicable (not punitive)	No, nothing is *due,* to measure out, (to achieve Justice)
JUSTICE ABOVE LAW (RECTIFYING, JUST MERCIES) Split Arc **B** Jus → Love Acts of Mercy that Achieve Justice; satisfying some real need, lack, or right, often a Human Right); Is sometimes known as Social Justice. Better term is *Biblical Justice.* Captured in story of Good Samaritan, or in general, systematic acts of caring for the needy. (Voluntary; State is not the main actor).	Right: Yes Legal Duty: No (God and Conscience alone may supply a duty, not Law; Moral Obligation; Good Samaritan)	**Is Justice** Exceeds a Legal Duty, *Maximalist*	**Voluntary Acts of Justice (Restorative, Rectifying, Private)** **Actors: Private: Yes State: No?** (State is not essentially involved in supplying it. State can give discretionary aid in some ways.) **Examples:** Good Samaritans, Corrie Ten Boom (Individuals), Charities, Capacity Building (non-St.), Private Aid Givers, NGOs helping people.	Inapplicable (not punitive); **However:** State can enforce laws against private actors and itself if causing harm, or violating laws in rendering services. **Examples:** If a Good Samaritan fails to save, she isn't typically punished, but State can punish her for causing new harm; it can also enforce safety code violations against a soup kitchen.	Yes, aid is measurable, and given to restore, make whole, redress injustices (achieves Justice)

JUSTICE IN LAW (LEGAL JUSTICE) — Straight Line **A** — Js→Law→is→Love. Rights and Duties Are Recognized and Enforced at Law; Legally Compulsory. **Kinds:**		Is Justice (In Traditional Sense)	Positive, Providing Side of Justice. By Kinds, Actors:	Negative, Punitive Side of Justice. By Kinds, Actors:	Amount, *Positive and Negative Sides*
i) Human Rights (HRs) (inherent; have as a human; coming from God; life, liberty, speech, association, conscience, religion, etc.)	Legal Rights: Yes / Legal Duties: Yes / In each kind, i, ii, iii, Legal Rights and Duties *correspond* with each other / (State enforces corresponding rights and duties, if not privately satisfied.)	Give to each his due and don't violate or withhold his rights, in accordance with what Law/State requires. **Minimalist** / Doing this achieves the basic Minimum of Justice (the **BOTTOM LINE OF JUSTICE**, which no one should go below)	i) HR: Yes, Applicable. Actors: Private: Yes State: Yes (All should *Satisfy HRs.* BUT, those going above a legal duty to do so are in another category, Section B above.) (State can sometimes *articulate* HRs, but does not create them)	i) HR: State is the main vindicator of violations.	i) HR: Yes
ii) Civil Rights (CRs) (Via Constitutions, Statutes, Regs., etc.)			ii) CR: Yes, Applicable. Actors: Private: Yes State: Yes (State and Private actors should satisfy Civil Rights. State creates and/or articulates CRs)	ii) CR: State is the main enforcer, vindicator of violations.	ii) CR: Yes
iii) Various Legal Rights (VLRs) (i.e., Torts, Contracts, Inheritance, Property, Family Law, Entities, Due Process Rights, etc.)			iii) VLR: Yes, Applicable. Actors: Private: Yes State: Yes? (State less so. Chiefly Private fulfillment, in contracts, duties of care, inheritances, etc.) (State less commonly satisfying rights, duties here, but usually enforcing breaches of same)	iii) VLR: State is main enforcer. (Sometimes Private enforcement systems exist: i.e., mediation, arbitration, often with State supervision.)	iii) VLR: Yes

INJUSTICE BELOW THIS LINE (JUSTICE ABOVE IT)

CHAPTER 3

LOVE, JUSTICE, LAW

³⁵One of them, an expert in the law, tested him with this question:
³⁶"Teacher, which is the greatest commandment in the Law?" ³⁷Jesus
replied: "'Love the Lord your God with all your heart and with all
your soul and with all your mind.' ³⁸This is the first and greatest com-
mandment. ³⁹And the second is like it: 'Love your neighbor as yourself.'
⁴⁰All the Law and the Prophets hang on these two commandments."
(Matthew 22:35-40)

⁹The commandments, "You shall not commit adultery," "You shall not
murder," "You shall not steal," "You shall not covet," and whatever other
command there may be, are summed up in this one command: "Love your
neighbor as yourself." ¹⁰Love does no harm to a neighbor. Therefore love
is the fulfillment of the law.
(Romans 13:9-10)

For the entire law is fulfilled in keeping this one command: "Love your
neighbor as yourself."
(Galatians 3:14)

Introduction: Love, Justice And Law

IF LOVE IS the greatest command God has given us, that is to love God and our
neighbors as ourselves, what does that have to do with justice? Is there a relationship between *love* and *justice*; and how does *law* fit into it? Yes, there is a relationship between *love* and *justice*, and with *law* also: When justice is done toward our

neighbor, it means we are treating that person right, and this is a type of loving him or her. Some of that justice is effectuated (implemented) through State law (civil government); some of it is not (remember the story of the Good Samaritan?). If the law is good and just to begin with (Right), and is properly followed, it means we are treating our neighbors rightly (justly) through implementing that law, and again, that shows them love.

A simple example of a traffic light placed at a busy and dangerous intersection in a city should illustrate the point. Suppose that intersection has seen lots of accidents, some life-threatening. Suppose also the city council met, and after discussion, it passed a law requiring the installation of a traffic light at the intersection. The new law saves lives and prevents accidents. This act of justice done by the city, via its law, is loving to its inhabitants.

If law can be a way of loving our neighbors, by effecting some justice toward them, I suppose it makes sense to give a working definition of *law*. In scouring scholarship and Christian thought on this over time, I suggest a simple summary definition of Law could be this: *Rules of human conduct for a more just and flourishing society, including appropriate consequences for violating same.*

"To love" truly is the greatest command among humans, and it may be said that if everyone did that, we would have less need of written laws to show and command us how to treat one another (we would be doing justice and living rightly with our neighbor by following the command to love them – specifics as to how to flesh that out in context would come later).

Love is *abstract* in one sense, serving as the *emotional motivator* for doing justice and treating people right in the first place. Justice similarly has its abstract side of good substantive standards to live by. Love and justice each also has its *concrete*, implementing side too. When we implement justice, either through law or above it, and so treat our fellow man rightly, we see a concrete example of actual justice taking shape; and this is also a concrete example of showing them love (i.e., justice and love become tangible, actualized). This helps build a better society. So, implementing good (godly) law is one way of making justice and love concrete and real for our neighbors. This is doing justice in and through the law, and in legal systems. But it is not the only way, as indicated above and below.

The Basic Diagram

The following diagram seeks to put these ideas of law, love, justice and rights together into a single summary illustration showing their connections. In it you will see three kinds of lines. Line A, the straight, horizontal line, shows justice done *in and through* law. Line B, the first arc, shows, justice done *above* the law (Good Samaritans). Line C, the highest arc, shows love that is not likely satisfying justice or any real human needs. Each line also corresponds to Sections A, B, and C in Table 2.1 in Chapter 2, and is even shown as mini-icons in separate text boxes in that table (see above).

The three ledger boxes (rectangles) in the lower left half of Diagram 3.1, are also marked A, B, and C, and staggered, aligning with the lines they help describe (they explain some characteristics of each line). [36]

The result of improving justice and righteousness, is greater joy and peace (Romans 14:17), shown in the lower right side circle.

See after this diagram, specific, detailed explanations to help walk you through it.

---

[36] Similar to the three strata in Table 2.1 the three ledgers here are also arranged in ascending order (C, B, A) from the minimalist (bottom) to maximalist (highest) approaches to human conduct and justice. (Diagram 3.1 and Table 2.1 are vitally interconnected.)

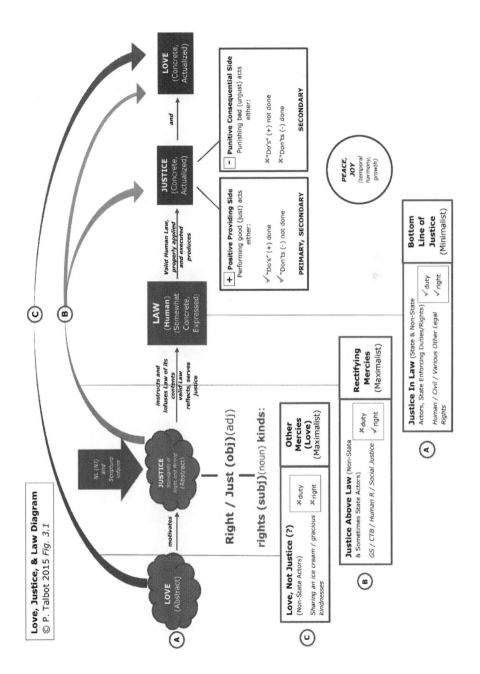

Love, Justice, & Law Diagram
© P. Talbot 2015 Fig. 3.1

Explanation of Love, Justice, Law Diagram

I. The straight horizontal line (A) shows the most straightforward interpretation of how love, justice, and law relate in legal systems.[37] On the left side, we start with Love (in its abstract sense, as an emotion), motivating good conduct, i.e., Justice (in its abstract sense, as just standards). (These abstract sides of Love and Justice are shown in clouds.) Continuing in line A, sometimes the standards of Justice go into laws, and legal systems, infusing them with just content (shown in the square of Law, in the middle). Implementation of those good and just laws results in actual Justice being done (in its concrete sense), and this is loving one's neighbor (an actual concrete example of love; the concrete sides of Love and Justice are shown in solid squares).

The sources of standards of Justice are shown as (i) Natural Law ("NL": a kind of *general revelation*, including about moral truth, implanted in us (in our consciences) by God, when creating us in His image, and discoverable by normal thinking, yet which can be clouded by sin), and (ii) Scripture (*special revelation*, including a more specific revelation of moral truth than is visible in NL).[38]

In the diagram, see also how the *objective* aspect of Justice, as "Right," and the *subjective*, specific rights stemming from it, are shown within the context of

---

[37] And in any social institutions having similar internal "legal systems"; i.e., those having internal "laws" and rules in their administration and structure (such as hospitals, schools, churches, corporations, and so on).

[38] NL is said to be those moral truths "we can't not know." J. BUDZISZEWSKI, WRITTEN ON THE HEART, THE CASE FOR NATURAL LAW 61 (1997) (interpreting St. Augustine on the subject). Its primary principles are very general; e.g., humans should do good, avoid evil, love their neighbor, and protect life; also, secondary principles can be derived from these by exercising proper reason. *Id.*, at 61, 109. *See also Ps.* 19; *Pr.* 8:10-11; *Rom.* 1:19, 2:14-15 (verses supporting NL). Scripture contains more specifics than NL, but it takes skill in interpreting its principles of justice for society today – a subject discussed in the next chapter. NL is commonly said to consist of the Ten Commandments and/ or the general moral principles underlying them. *See generally, id.* at 109, 202-204.

Natural Justice (NJ) is standards to which we can be held accountable because they are just, regardless of human consensus. *See id.* at 40-41. *Natural Rights* (NR) are rights we receive from God as our Creator, and which government is charged with protecting; they are to be enjoyed consistently with the moral requirements of NL, and are similar to a correct concept of human rights, today (see above). *Id.* at 112-116.

Justice. The Positive and Negative (Punitive) sides of *legal Justice* are also shown in the concrete side of the diagram. This summarizes legal justice.

The fruit of this increase in actual Justice (righteousness) in society is greater Peace (Isaiah 32:17) and Joy (Romans 14:17).[39]

II. The first arc (B) shows Justice being done above and beyond State civil (or similar) legal systems and duties, as illustrated in the story of the Good Samaritan, above. Skipping over formal law, this still results in actual Justice, and Love, and increased Peace and Joy.

III. The high arc (C) depicts loving acts of kindness that may go beyond the scope of Justice, and any rights or duties associated with it, as discussed above.

In sum, God wants us to love Him and our neighbors. We can love our neighbors by acting with justice toward them. Sometimes, we can do this justice through law, in more formal legal systems. Sometimes, we can show them justice, still serving their needs and rights, by going above what the law requires. And sometimes, love just stands on its own. All three approaches have been shared in this information. *It's important to remember as Christian students and attorneys, we have to seek God in improving justice in our legal systems (line A)*, while still doing the important things in B, and C also.

DISCUSSION QUESTIONS:

1. How is justice sometimes also love? What is the relationship between love, law and justice?

---

[39] *The fruit of that righteousness will be peace, its effect will be quietness and confidence forever. Is.* 32:17 (Augustine similarly stressed this result of justice); *For the kingdom of God is . . . a matter of . . . righteousness, peace, and joy in the Holy Spirit. . . . Romans* 14:17 (among several Scriptures showing such a connection of righteousness and justice, to joy).

31

2. Who is your neighbor, and how can you show love or justice to your neighbor this week?

3. As a Christian student, attorney, educator, or justice advocate, in what ways can you suggest improvements in justice, coming through your legal system?

PRAYER POINTS:

1. Pray that you would love your neighbor as yourself.
2. Pray for opportunities to do justice with love at your university or work.
3. Pray for your lawmakers to make good laws that do not violate standards of true justice (as Right and godly), but that fulfill them, and *pray for your involvement in that lawmaking process.*

Chapter 4

SCRIPTURAL AND SECULAR SCHOOLS OF JURISPRUDENCE

[17]Do not think that I have come to abolish the Law or the Prophets;
I have not come to abolish them but to fulfill them.
[18]For truly I tell you, until heaven and earth disappear, not the smallest
letter, not the least stroke of a pen, will by any means disappear from the
Law until everything is accomplished.
(Matthew 5:17-18)

We demolish arguments and every pretension that sets itself up against the
knowledge of God, and we take captive every thought to make it obedient
to Christ.
(2 Corinthians 10:5)

IN ORDER TO understand the substance of justice, and its incorporation into law, scholars have come up with *schools of thought* on law, also called *schools of jurisprudence,* or views of legal philosophy. For instance, I have given a definition of *law* above and how it interrelates with *justice, rights,* and *love,* in a classical Christian tradition. A comprehensive annotated table is available in Appendix IV (Table 4.1), which summarizes various schools of thought about law and justice (jurisprudence, but not in the sense of case law), in some detail.

Scriptural Schools

Some schools of jurisprudence reflect a more biblical approach, like the first two in annotated Table 4.1 (Appendix IV). This includes *Scripture* itself (*special revelation*), and what it says about law and justice, and secondly, *Natural Law* (*NL*, and a part of *general revelation*).

1. Scripture is *special revelation* from God. It has a lot to say about law and justice, yet some issues can arise. It's important to know, for instance, how much of the OT and its very strict laws should apply in societies today.

It is insufficient and incorrect to simply say all the OT law was only for Israel, and doesn't apply today, since Jesus, the NT, and the Church have arrived on the scene. Things like the Ten Commandments (thou shall not kill, steal, commit adultery, covet, etc.) also do apply today. In many States, such commands are incorporated into their civil law, and should be. Jesus also affirmed much of the OT law (Matthew 5:17-18). Some good OT laws were intended to apply both within and outside Israel, universally, to humankind, unlimited by geography and time.

It is equally incorrect, however, to suggest all OT laws in Israel should simply be incorporated directly and literally into all societies and legal systems.[40] Since God gave the law to Israel, it is supposedly His will for all nations in history (so that idea goes).

This section is intended to help you navigate between these two extreme approaches.

Two common, sensible approaches to incorporation of Scriptural laws, are called, **Repeated Unless Repeated** (RR – a *dispensational* approach), and **Maintained Unless Modified** (MM – a so-called *reformed* approach).[41] In the RR view, scholars say the OT law *does not apply* to specific situations today unless Jesus (or the NT) specifically so incorporates it. See, however, in Matthew 5:17-18 (above in this chapter), where Jesus seems to do just that, in sweeping terms. In the MM

---

[40] This approach is also called *Reconstructionism* (some inaccurately call it *theocracy* (*lit.* "God's rule")). It has some variations, and is a minority view among Christian scholars.

[41] *Dispensationalists* generally see God's covenant history with Israel and humankind more in separate stages (dispensations); while *Reformed* scholars (i.e., Calvinists) see greater continuity between the Covenants and history.

view, scholars hold that OT law applies today, in some sectors of society, unless Jesus or NT Scriptures say differently (i.e., by modifying OT law). Given the strength of Jesus' words in Matthew 5:17-18, and in similar passages, the MM view seems the best one. However, it's not clear that RR or MM would render very different results on important issues, given Jesus' incorporating words in such passages.

Some things certainly have changed between the Old and New Covenants (OT and NT). Knowing how biblical law should apply in societies today is a very important issue because of those changes.[42] Some things in the OT law intended for Israel may still apply in societies (including civil government) today, but sometimes this may be under a different social institution's jurisdiction than the State's (in the case of Israel). Such institutions include the Church, the family, schools, and others. Each of these may employ different means of punishment than Israel was commanded to use for violations in its capacity as a State (i.e., these institutions should not wield the deadly power of the sword – they aren't States). To illustrate, cursing one's parents is still wrong, as it was in the OT, but it may not end in capital punishment if it is under the jurisdiction of the family today, whereas it could have in ancient Israel, as a State.

A good, general, guiding principle is that if a law in the OT applied not only *inside ancient Israel*, but also *outside* it, then it should apply *since* ancient Israel, in societies today (it's a universal and continuous law; like not sacrificing one's children, killing the innocent, stealing, and so on).[43]

Knowing how to apply biblical OT law in societies today is greatly aided by seeing important distinctions in three kinds of OT law: (i) the **moral law** (i.e., in the Ten Commandments and others; i.e., thou shall not kill, steal, etc.); (ii) the **civil law** (illustrations or cases in law, as in specific applications of the moral law; i.e., covering a pit one has dug, or remedies for a slave who has his tooth knocked out); and (iii) the **ceremonial law** (ritual and religious worship

---

[42] We know obeying the OT law (and even specific NT rules) cannot save us eternally, but they have value in contributing toward justice, joy and peace in society, giving us illustrations of what it means to love others, and shows us our need of a Savior from our sins. *See Galatians* 3:10-11, 21-25.

[43] From the teachings of Dr. Joseph Kickasola, Biblical Law class (1993), Regent University School of Law (notes on file with the author).

laws, including dietary and tabernacle/temple sacrificial rules, and ceremonial cleanliness).

The first two apply today, but in different ways, while the ceremonial law largely does not apply since Christ has done away with the sacrificial system by the sacrifice of Himself, and has established the Church, with its new kind of worship in Spirit and in truth, and its sacraments (see John 4:23 and Hebrews 10:11-14).

In short, as a saying, the more general an OT law is (i.e., thou shall not steal) the easier it is to apply, assuming people can agree on what stealing is. However the more specific an OT law is, in its wording and context (i.e., do not cook a young goat in its mother's milk), the harder it is to apply; it usually has only an indirect application.

In some cases, it is of course true that even a very specific OT moral law or case illustration can apply directly to a situation today. But this is when the current situation is the same situation being described in the OT civil law's illustration (if not modified by Jesus or the NT). In that case, very specific moral prohibitions in the OT law should apply equally and correctly to the same specific situations happening today. A good illustration might be OT laws on sexual immorality. If Scripture says adultery, homosexual activity, sex with animals, and incest, are immoral and illegal, then the same situations in societies today are also immoral, and Scriptural edicts against such improprieties should apply with equal vigor to the same situations happening currently.[44] Again, this holds true for *morally grounded* specific illustrations in OT *civil* law, and especially those that applied beyond Israel's borders; but is not true (or is inapplicable) for specific illustrations found in the *ceremonial* law.

In contrast, if a specific OT illustration does not correlate with or describe a situation at hand, it may still be instructive, yet it applies only indirectly. In such cases (i.e., see some of the examples above, and numerous similar ones, such as *paying restitution for a goring ox*, or *not yoking different animals together*, and so on), significant relevance should still exist on moral

---

[44] The severity of punishment and those having jurisdiction to enforce it are other matters to consider in the era after ancient Israel (see the Handbook on this).

issues for civil society today. However, such illustrations *simply do not apply literally and directly.* Again for example, I may not have a goring ox, but I may have a reckless son or employee; similarly, I may not have a loose ax head that could fly off and kill someone, but if I use dangerous equipment in work, I should keep it maintained, and pay compensation if I carelessly injure another with it.

At least two interpretive aids can be very helpful in applying such indirectly relevant OT illustrations to current social issues: (i) **analogizing** from specific OT illustrations to situations at hand (i.e., building a railing atop of your roof in OT law is akin to requiring installation of safety fences around a swimming pool, and has additional similar safety applications for today, including in automobile and consumer goods manufacturing); and/or (ii) ascertaining the generally applicable, **underlying moral principles** *behind* the specific illustrations or commands, (like sanctity of life and property, improving safety, or paying compensation for an injury one has caused), and then **applying** any relevant ones to a situation at hand. This should be doable in a reasonably straightforward way, and the reader should verify this when reading and thinking about such illustrations in Scripture. This diagram (Fig. 4.1) summarizes these approaches.

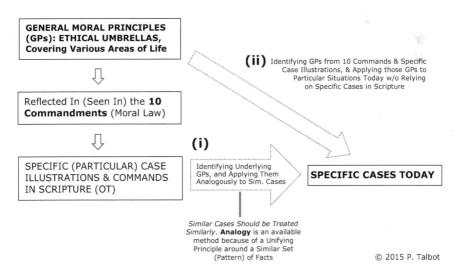

Fig 4.1. Two means of applying OT biblical law today

*Severity of **punishments** is also a very important issue.* Punishments may differ from Israel's OT law and today. Also, who administers such punishments, in terms of having jurisdiction, has also changed in some cases; i.e., from the State to the Church (as in issues of idolatry, blasphemy, and sorcery), or from State to the family (as in disciplining children who dishonor their parents), and so on. Some violations of moral law may of course only get punished directly by God (outside of any human jurisdiction, instead of in and through it). This may be done either by His own temporal means of doing so, or in the end, eternally in judgment. (See a fuller discussion of these matters in the Student Handbook.)

2. A second biblically-sourced school of jurisprudence is Christian-based Natural Law (NL). As noted, this is considered part of God's general revelation to humans, and is a kind of moral imprint and code of His standards. NL is something God has put in the human heart and conscience, and is knowable and accessible to us in our intellects and conscience, since we are created in God's image. It is not *written*, except on our hearts and intellects (see Romans 2:14-15). NL is always complementary to Scripture (it may not contradict it). NL existed prior to Scripture, operates with and within it, sometimes interpreting, or being interpreted by it, and is still applicable since Scripture.[45] This diagram (Fig 4.2) shows its basic structure (see more on this in the Student Handbook.)[46]

---

[45] Scripture actually makes express, in written form, many general precepts of NL. The Student Handbook covers this topic in greater detail.

[46] Adapted from J. BUDZISZEWSKI, NATURAL LAW FOR LAWYERS 70 (2006). The three levels of precepts are, 1) the intuitively obvious (e.g., not injuring the innocent), 2) those most already know (corresponding roughly to the Ten Commandments; Luther even considered these ten to be the perfect expression of NL), 3) those needing more thought to see (corresponding to other examples in the OT Law). *Id.* at 73-74. In the diagram, *Conclusions* are things inherently wrong (killing someone by careless driving). *Determinations* are things deemed wrong according to specific customs in law (driving on the left vs. right side of the road). *Id.* at 84.

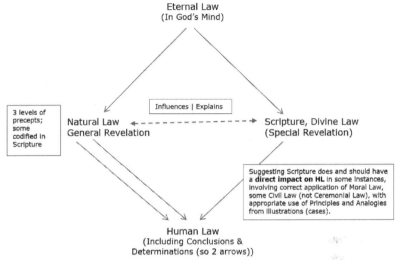

Fig. 4.2. A Christian View of the NL (Aquinas, and after)

Secular Schools

Other schools in Appendix IV (Table 4.1) are more secular, and incomplete. These include the schools of **Legal Positivism**, **Historical** and **Sociological Jurisprudence**, **Legal Realism**, **Critical Legal Studies** (and its offshoots, such as **Critical Race**, **Gender**, or **Gay Jurisprudence**), and the more recent school of **Law and Economics** (a utilitarian school, sometimes placing costs above ethics). Instead of detailing these schools here (in the text), study Appendix IV, and its shorter version (Table 4.2) at the end of this chapter, which supplies a succinct introduction on each of these schools.[47]

Some of these secular schools may reflect truths found in Scripture to some degree. In other ways, they may be very hostile and against Scripture and a Christian worldview. In the charts given, as in history, you should see a growing trend away from honoring God's moral truths in the above Scriptural schools

---

[47] Table 4.2 is a more condensed, succinct (one-page) version of Table 4.1 (Appendix IV), and is sufficient as a short introduction. This short table is the work of Professor Roger Bern (a mentor, deceased), except for the last column on Law and Economics, which I added because it emerged as a dominant school sometime after Prof. Bern's initial analysis (any other alterations by this author, to his initial chart, are shown in brackets).

of jurisprudence, toward an increasing moral relativism in jurisprudence. Sadly, this indicates a sliding away from the moral foundations of law in many societies.

For instance, in the shorter chart (Table 4.2) note the fixed, uniform and universal characteristics of moral principles embedded in law, seen in its highest standards (capturing the view of England's Sir. William Blackstone's (d. 1780)). The table shows such grand moral characteristics starting on the left side, and traces their erosion with increasing relativism over time, moving toward the right side.[48] Notice also the table describes earlier Christian views of NL (Aquinas), as well as the later secularized distortions of it.

This slide toward moral relativism in law is increasing in many places in the world. *Islamist extremism* in jurisprudence is also an increasing concern, showing up as an extreme on the other side of the spectrum. I hope you can identify such problems in jurisprudence and law and contribute some real solutions.

DISCUSSION QUESTIONS:

1. What are the distinctions between moral law, civil law (including its moral case illustrations), and ceremonial law in the OT? How do such distinctions help us decide which OT laws should still apply today, and which should not?

2. How should specific case illustrations in the OT's civil law apply in societies today (if at all)? What sorts of principles and interpretative approaches should help you in doing that? (name some)

---

[48] *See id.* (Table 4.2).

3. Identify some issues in your society or its justice systems which you think could benefit from the inclusion or influence of Scriptural moral laws? What strategies would you use to help make that happen (would you have to identify such Scriptures by actual verses in your strategy)?

PRAYER POINTS:

1. Pray Romans 12:2 and 2 Corinthians 10:5 that you would not conform to the pattern of this world, but be transformed by the renewing of your mind, and take captive every stray thought in jurisprudence, and make it obedient to Christ.
2. Pray for your legal and justice systems to adopt God's standards of justice and pray for your colleagues to not be conformed to this world, but to also be transformed in their thinking.
3. Pray Psalm 1 to delight in the law of the Lord and meditate on his law, and not to walk in the way of sinners and scoffers, but to stand firm.

Table 4.2 WHAT IS LAW? A general definition: "A rule of action which is prescribed by some superior, and which the inferior is bound to obey." Blackstone / © 2004 Roger Bern, Liberty U. School of Law

	NATURAL LAW						
BIBLICAL	**ENLIGHTENMENT**	**EVOLUTIONARY**	**LEGAL POSITIVISM**	**SOCIOLOGICAL (HISTORICAL)**	**LEGAL REALISM (PRAGMATISM)**	**CRITICAL LEGAL STUDIES**	**LAW AND ECONOMICS**
SOURCE OF LAW: Created by God	Inherent in Nature		Created by Government	Contemporary Society (or Historical Practices)	Judge who Decides		Society, Markets
LAW / GOD		(GOD)	(GOD)	(GOD)	(GOD)	(GOD)	(GOD?)
[Swift v. Tyson (1842)]					[Erie v. Tompkins (1938)]	(LAW)	$, Profit max., human wants
HOW IS LAW REVEALED OR DETERMINED? Revealed by God in:	Discovered by Reason	Determined by Evolutionary Forces	Statutes enacted because of conscious thinking [But see Nuremberg Trials]	Take a poll, or ask experts (e.g., sociologists) or search historic practices	Judge's decisions-case law	Justice without law (not *above* it, but excluding law)	Wealth maximization; Utility, Efficiency
1. Consciousness and Nature [Reason] Ps 19:1-4 Rom 1:19-20; 2:15 Col 1:16-17	("Collective General Will" – Rousseau)	But man resists an evolutionary, deterministic state of affairs. Although control by man over his "law" is inconsistent with evolutionary principles, proponents assert man can overcome the forces of evolution because he is a special kind of reasoning being. Thus he should be able to use his reason to determine and direct the evolving law order		Georgia Sodomy case (1986) Texas Sodomy case (2003) Polygamy case (1878) Mass. Homosexual marriage case (2003)	Law [△] Cases [Read the cases and develop rule from series of cases] No "law" until a case decision	But some social engineering by gov't until society arrives at "solidarity" or harmony (FAMILY) Social Interests (Implications) vs. Case at hand	Seeking greatest good for most people, not always interested in articulated legal rights, promises and obligations in individual cases
2. Bible Ex 20:1-17 Dt 30:15-20 Ps 147:19-20 II Tim 3:16 (Blackstone, Aquinas – No "law" passed by gov't contrary to God's law is law at all) Role of Judge (Ex 18:15-16) Law [▽] → Cases				Roscoe Pound observed the dilemma: How to convince the public that the law was something fixed and settled, whose authority was beyond question, while at the same time making constant readjustments and sometimes radical changes in response to changing desires?			*Efficient Breaches* Selling babies?
CHARACTERISTICS OF THE TYPES OF LAW							
(FIXED) Matt 5:18; Gen 3 (Fall)	[FIXED]	(FIXED)	(FIXED)	(FIXED)	(FIXED)	(NO LAW)	(FIXED?)
(UNIFORM) Josh 9:3-9; 15, 18-20	[UNIFORM]	(UNIFORM)	(UNIFORM)	(UNIFORM)	(UNIFORM)	(NO LAW)	(UNIFORM?)
(UNIVERSAL) Acts 17:26-27	[UNIVERSAL]	(UNIVERSAL)	(UNIVERSAL)	(UNIVERSAL)	(UNIVERSAL)	(NO LAW)	(UNIVERSAL)

PART II

ON LAW AND SOCIETY (GOVERNMENT)

CHAPTER 5

SCRIPTURE AND GOVERNMENT

*¹Let everyone be subject to the governing authorities, for there is no author-
ity except that which God has established. The authorities that exist
have been established by God. ²Consequently, whoever rebels against the
authority is rebelling against what God has instituted, and those who do
so will bring judgment on themselves. ³For rulers hold no terror for those
who do right, but for those who do wrong. Do you want to be free from
fear of the one in authority? Then do what is right and you will be com-
mended. ⁴For the one in authority is God's servant for your good. But if
you do wrong, be afraid, for rulers do not bear the sword for no reason.
They are God's servants, agents of wrath to bring punishment on the
wrongdoer. ⁵Therefore, it is necessary to submit to the authorities, not only
because of possible punishment but also as a matter of conscience. ⁶This
is also why you pay taxes, for the authorities are God's servants, who give
their full time to governing. ⁷Give to everyone what you owe them: If you
owe taxes, pay taxes; if revenue, then revenue; if respect, then respect; if
honor, then honor.*
(Romans 13:1-7)⁴⁹

Righteousness exalts a nation, but sin condemns any people.
(Proverbs 14:34)

---

⁴⁹ *See also* 1 *Peter* 2:13-17; *Titus* 3:1 (saying similarly).

SCRIPTURE TELLS US many things about government.[50]

(1) Scripture shows us that all government and authority ultimately comes from God, as seen in Romans 13 above. In the chapters above, we discussed ideas of law and justice. These are things administered to a significant degree by the State (again meaning the civil government at any level). As will be seen below, however, law and justice, in their broader definitions above, may also be administered in less formal governing structures (i.e., fathers in families, bosses at work, pastors in churches, teachers in school, and so on). The State is not the only authority in society, nor the only one in contemplation within God's plan for a more just society.

(2) The primary purpose of government, with its administration of law and justice, is to restrain sin on the earth since man is fallen, and thus to bless people. Augustine and Luther supported this view.[51]

(3) Students sometimes assume the Romans passage above and ones like it teach blind obedience to governing authority. That is incorrect. Notice Romans 13:4 imposes conditions and duties on the State, as well on its citizens. It must act as God's agent and servant for our good, commending that good, and punishing wrongdoing. When the State, or any governing authority commands us to sin, we are obligated to obey God, rather than man (or that authority), even if we suffer unjust punishments for doing so (see Acts 4:18; 5:29; Daniel 6:10; Exodus 1:17 (Hebrew midwives); Esther 4:14).

(4) God rules ultimately over all the nations of the earth, and their leaders. He can and does tear them down for disobedience, and exalts others according to righteousness in His sovereign plan. God is sovereign over all nations and kingdoms. He even establishes the locations and boundaries of nations and their times (Acts 17:26; Deuteronomy. 32:8; and see Genesis. 10 (table of nations)).

(5) Some will be concerned then, asking why does God allow evil men and tyrants to come into power (or even ordain it)? Recall that God is sovereign over this, and will use it for His ultimate purposes and His glory. Calvin, or those

---

[50] In addition to Scriptures here, see Appendices I, V, VI. For an expansion of the short summary points here, and more Scriptures, see the separate Student Handbook.

[51] *See* JOHN EIDSMOE, GOD AND CAESAR, BIBLICAL FAITH AND POLITICAL ACTION 15 (Wipf and Stock Publ. 1997).

sympathetic with his views, also taught that a people usually gets the kind of government they ought to, either a wicked or honorable one, according to their deeds (a kind of *deserving* of it, or simply a reaping of what was sown).[52]

Some Scriptures touching upon these and related issues are listed here, and organized by subject categories, as headings. Appendix V in this Study Guide also lists Scriptures discussing wisdom principles for godly government. (Please see and study the Scriptures in this Appendix.)

The Dominion Mandate [Initial Grounds for Governing Anything]

Genesis 1:28. *God blessed them and said to them, "Be fruitful and increase in number; fill the earth and subdue it. Rule over the fish in the sea and the birds in the sky and over every living creature that moves on the ground."*

Genesis 9:1-2, 7. (Similar, said to Noah.)

God Is Source of Government, Purpose Is Justice, Serves As His Agent

Romans 13:1-7. (See text above.)

1 Peter 2:13-17. *[13] Submit yourselves for the Lord's sake to every human authority: whether to the emperor, as the supreme authority, [14] or to governors, who are sent by him to punish those who do wrong and to commend those who do right. [15] For it is God's will that by doing good you should silence the ignorant talk of foolish people . . . [17] Show proper respect to everyone . . . honor the emperor.*

Titus 3:1. *Remind the people to be subject to the rulers and authorities, to be obedient, to be ready to do whatever is good,*

---

[52] *See* Bill Muehlenberg, *Calvin on Wicked Rulers and God's Judgment*, CULTURE WATCH BLOG (Feb. 27, 2016), https://billmuehlenberg.com/2016/02/27/calvin-on-wicked-rulers-and-gods-judgment/; Muehlenberg, *On Getting the Government We Deserve*, CULTURE WATCH BLOG (Feb. 23, 2016), https://billmuehlenberg.com/2016/02/23/on-getting-the-government-we-deserve/ (a more specific discussion on *deserving*); *See also Why Does God Allow Evil Men Like Hitler and Saddam to Come Into Power?*, GOT QUESTIONS, https://www.gotquestions.org/Hitler-Saddam.html (last visited July 28, 2018). Study also the doctrine of *concurrence*. This link from Ligonier Ministries should help get you started: http://www.ligonier.org/learn/devotionals/providence-and-evil/.

God Establishes Nations

Acts 17:26. *From one man he [God] made all the nations, that they should inhabit the whole earth; and he [God] marked out their appointed times in history and the boundaries of their lands.*

Deuteronomy 32:8. *When the Most High gave the nations their inheritance, when he divided all mankind, he set up boundaries for the peoples according to the number of the sons of Israel.*

Genesis 10. (See whole chapter; table of nations.)

Obeying Authority

Romans 13:2, 5-6. (See text above.)

Titus 3:1. (See text above.)

1 Peter 2:13-14. (See text above.)

Yet, Obeying God Over Men

Acts 4:19. *But Peter and John replied, "Which is right in God's eyes: to listen to you, or to him? You be the judges! . . . "*

Acts 5:29. *Peter and the other apostles replied: "We must obey God rather than human beings! . . ."*

God's Sovereignty Over Nations and Rulers (Exalting or Removing)

1 Kings 19:15-16. *[15]The LORD said to him, "Go back the way you came, and go to the Desert of Damascus. When you get there, anoint Hazael king over Aram [a foreign nation]. [16]Also, anoint Jehu son of Nimshi king over Israel, and anoint Elisha son of Shaphat from Abel Meholah to succeed you as prophet.*

Proverbs 14:34. *Righteousness exalts a nation, but sin condemns any people.*

Jeremiah 18:6-10. *[6]He said, "Can I not do with you, Israel, as this potter does?" declares the LORD. "Like clay in the hand of the potter, so are you in my hand, Israel. [7]If at any time I announce that a nation or kingdom is to be uprooted, torn down and destroyed, [8]and if that nation I warned repents of its evil, then I will relent and not inflict on it the disaster I had planned. [9]And if at another time I announce that a nation or kingdom is to be built up and planted, [10]and if it does evil in my sight and does not obey me, then I will reconsider the good I had intended to do for it."*

Daniel 2:21a. *He changes times and seasons; he deposes kings and raises up others.*

Daniel 4:17b. *". . .so that the living may know that the Most High is sovereign over all kingdoms on earth and gives them to anyone he wishes and sets over them the lowliest of people."* (See also Daniel 4:25; 5:21 (setting over kingdoms *anyone He pleases*).)

See also Isaiah (especially 10, 13-23, 41-47), Jeremiah (especially 25-27, 46-51), Amos 1, Ezekiel 17; 1 Kings 19; 2 Kings 8-9 (similar selections).

Matthew 28:18. *Then Jesus came to them and said, "All authority in heaven and on earth has been given to me . . ."*

Colossians 1:18. *And he is the head of the body, the church; he is the beginning and the firstborn from among the dead, so that in everything he might have the supremacy.*

Sovereignty, Evil Dictators and Nations

Exodus 7:3-4. *³But I will harden Pharaoh's heart, and though I multiply my signs and wonders in Egypt, ⁴he will not listen to you. . . .*

Exodus 9:12. *But the LORD hardened Pharaoh's heart and he would not listen to Moses and Aaron, just as the LORD had said to Moses. (see also Exodus 14:8 (same)).*

Proverbs 14:34. *Righteousness exalts a nation, but sin condemns any people* (supporting also the idea of nations getting the government they *deserve*).

Proverbs 16:4. *The LORD works out everything to its proper end— even the wicked for a day of disaster.*

Proverbs 21:1. *In the LORD's hand the king's heart is a stream of water that he channels toward all who please him.*

Isaiah 10:5, 12. *⁵Woe to the Assyrian, the rod of my anger, in whose hand is the club of my wrath! . . . ¹²When the Lord has finished all his work against Mount Zion and Jerusalem, he will say, "I will punish the king of Assyria for the willful pride of his heart and the haughty look in his eyes . . . ."*

Jeremiah 25:11-14. *¹¹This whole country will become a desolate wasteland, and these nations will serve the king of Babylon seventy years. ¹²"But when the seventy years are fulfilled, I will punish the king of Babylon and his nation, the land of the Babylonians, for their guilt,"* declares the LORD, *"and will make it desolate forever. ¹³I will bring on that land all the things I have spoken against it, all that are written in this book and prophesied by Jeremiah against all the nations. ¹⁴They themselves will be enslaved by many nations and great kings; I will repay them according to their deeds and the work of their hands."*

Jeremiah 27:5-7. *⁵With my great power and outstretched arm I made the earth and its people and the animals that are on it, and I give it to anyone I please. ⁶Now I will give all your countries into the hands of my servant Nebuchadnezzar king of Babylon; I will make even the wild animals subject to him. ⁷All nations will serve him and his son and his grandson until the time for his land comes; then many nations and great kings will subjugate him.*

Jeremiah 51:20, 23-25. ²⁰ *You are my war club, my weapon for battle— with you I shatter nations, with you I destroy kingdoms . . . ²³with you I shatter governors and officials. ²⁴Before your eyes I will repay Babylon and all who live in Babylonia for all the wrong they have done in Zion . . . . ²⁵I am against you, you destroying mountain, you who destroy the whole earth . . . . I will stretch out my hand against you, roll you off the cliffs, and make you a burned-out mountain.*

Habakkuk 1:6. *I am raising up the Babylonians, that ruthless and impetuous people, who sweep across the whole earth to seize dwellings not their own.*

James 1:13. *When tempted, no one should say, "God is tempting me." For God cannot be tempted by evil, nor does he tempt anyone . . . .* (God is innocent of governors' and rulers' wrongdoings.)

God's Hostility, and Punishing of, Disobedient Nations (Even After Establishing Them)

Genesis 15:16. *In the fourth generation your descendants will come back here, for the sin of the Amorites has not yet reached its full measure.* (They are not yet to be cast down.)

Psalm 2:1-2, 8-9. *¹Why do the nations conspire and the peoples plot in vain? ²The kings of the earth rise up and the rulers band together against the LORD and against his anointed . . . ⁸Ask me, and I will make the nations your inheritance, the ends of the earth your possession. ⁹You will break them with a rod of iron; you will dash them to pieces like pottery.*

Psalm 59:5, 8. ⁵ *God of Israel, rouse yourself to punish all the nations; show no mercy to wicked traitors. . . . ⁸But you laugh at them, LORD; you scoff at all those nations.*

Psalm 110:6. *He will judge the nations, heaping up the dead and crushing the rulers of the whole earth.*

Isaiah 8:9. *Raise the war cry, you nations, and be shattered! Listen, all you distant lands. Prepare for battle, and be shattered! Prepare for battle, and be shattered!*

Isaiah 34:2. *The LORD is angry with all nations; his wrath is on all their armies. He will totally destroy them, he will give them over to slaughter.*

Joel 3:2. *I will gather all nations and bring them down to the Valley of Jehoshaphat. There I will put them on trial for what they did to my inheritance, my people Israel . . . .* (See through verse 16 for the full context.)

Revelation 16:14,16. [14]*They are demonic spirits that perform signs, and they go out to the kings of the whole world, to gather them for the battle on the great day of God Almighty . . .* [16] *Then they gathered the kings together to the place that in Hebrew is called Armageddon.*

Revelation 19:15a, 19-20a. [15]*Coming out of his mouth is a sharp sword with which to strike down the nations. "He will rule them with an iron scepter." . . .* [19]*Then I saw the beast and the kings of the earth and their armies gathered together to wage war against the rider on the horse and his army.* [20]*But the beast was captured . . . .*

Godliness in Government

Proverbs 16:10. *The lips of a king speak as an oracle, and his mouth does not betray justice.*

(See Appendix V, "Scripture Verses from Proverbs on Good Governance," for additional Scriptural guidance.)

DISCUSSION QUESTIONS:

1. Who is the source of government? Who is the source of States and nations?

2. How can seeing God's sovereignty help us understand the hard situation of evil rulers in the earth? Does God promote sin (find a Scripture in the NT to answer this if you can)?

3. How do we continue to promote godliness in government and local leaders?

4. As a nation, what are the consequences of disobeying God's laws?

PRAYER POINTS:

1. Pray for your local leaders.
2. Pray for your national leaders.
3. Pray for the families of elected officials.
4. Pray for your own role in civil government.

CHAPTER 6

SOCIAL CONTRACT THEORY

They replied, "If today you will be a servant to these people and serve
them and give them a favorable answer, they will always be your servants."
(1 Kings 12:7)

GIVEN THAT LAW and justice are administered by the State and other governing authorities or institutions in society (including informal ones) it is now prudent to consider how society should be structured by such governing authorities, in the institutions in which they exist, to best achieve justice and blessing in a nation.

Social Contract (SK) theories are consent-based theories for the formation of civil society and governments, and have been very influential in the last couple centuries in shaping democracies around the world. They indicate some ideas on how governments should start, and to some degree how they should also be structured.

SK theories are valuable for their emphasis on the consent of the governed to their government, as a hedge against tyranny and for protection of liberties and rights. Some biblical support exists for this (see 1 Samuel 11:15 on the peoples' affirming selection of king Saul after God's choice, and 1 Kings 12, the rejection of king Rehoboam by most of Israel).

However, there are different kinds of SK theories (Locke, Hobbes, Rousseau, Kant, etc.) and these may either agree or disagree with biblical thinking to varying degrees. The structuring of society they suggest is also limited or incomplete.[53]

---

[53] See this author for a complete list of bibliographical references on all three thinkers. In general, see the *Stanford Encyclopedia of Philosophy*, and the *Internet Encyclopedia of Philosophy*, each available online.

I believe John Locke's view of the SK is one of the most helpful and bibli-cal models among other prolific theorists, (i.e., Hobbes and Rousseau), whom I rank behind him, in that order.[54] I say this for reasons I hope are self-evident in this Table. In short, each has his understanding of human nature, and something called the *State of Nature* (roughly meaning the state of humans' existence before deciding to organize into civil society and govern themselves, subject to varying interpretations as to when and how often that actually happened(s) in history; abbreviated, *SoN*, in this Table). Each thinker below has a different idea of what it means to be *in* and *to leave* the SoN.

[54] *See* Kim Ian Parker, *Locke, Religion, Rights, and the Rise of Modernity*, LUMEN 31, 115-29 (2012), *available at* https://www.erudit.org/en/journals/lumen/2012-v31-lumen0356/1013071ar.pdf.

Table 6.1. Comparison of Some Scholars on SK and the State of Nature (SoN)   © 2018 P. Talbot

Short Comparisons	Locke (1632-1704)	Hobbes (1588-1679)	Rousseau (1712-1778)
SoN, General Description & View of it:	Natural Law governs in SoN, but it's an unruly state; some individual justice. Civil Society is seen as a better way for humans than SoN SoN is short-lived	Brutish, intolerable: A harsh state of a "war of all against all." No moral compass is operating. SoN is very short-lived	Primitive, animal-like; Is seen as *ideal* state of man. Man is free, good, individualistic, and lives simply in nature. Civilization threatens it. SoN, too bad it's gone
State of Nature's Correlation with Historical-biblical record (Genesis)	SoN is real, not hypothetical; No specific time applies: anytime and place a gov't has not yet formed; i.e., American Indians at frontier Post Fall of Man, in which our human rights are susceptible to infringement due to sin.	Same, including also examples of American Indians, Civil War in England? Slightly vague Scriptural correlation. Likely post Fall of man: Example of Cain and Abel in later translation of Leviathan given as typifying this state of war (= post Fall)	Largely hypothetical SoN (conjectural human history). No attempt to correlate with Scripture; "Fall of man" *is* entering Civil Society. Inaccurate, rosy view of humans in SoN
Social Contract: Consent as Gov't legitimacy (Actual Contract)	Consent validates civil society and gov't; coercion is not allowed, except in rare circumstances; Consent is express or tacit	Consent is good; but gov't formed or seized by coercion and war is also alright. Consent is *not essential*	1st SK is oppressive (a class state), it protects propertied interests; 2nd SK is 100% consent of people, = only *valid state*, = "the Sovereign" (General Will)

Short Comparisons	Locke (1632-1704)	Hobbes (1588-1679)	Rousseau (1712-1778)
Intended function, role of Gov't (Civil Society)	Protection of Human (Natural) Rights, vindication of same; State is accountable, is a party to the Social K	Human survival; some rights sacrificed; State is not a party to the Social K	- Enforces the General Will (GW) of the Sovereign - Individual freedoms and rights are not enforced (all surrendered to Sovereign) - Gov't is *separate* from the Sovereign; it has an *Executive* role
Best Form of Government	Variable, but checks and balances is ideal (i.e., House of Lords, Commons, and King all existed in England); Representative gov't is best: interests and rights of people are first; Constitutional Monarchy is acceptable; his ideas on checks and balances influenced the American system	Variable, but prefers a strong King, a monarchy; tyranny is better than anarchy (any social order is better than none)	- 100% Pure Democracy on laws (all vote on it) - Coerced to follow the GW (legislative function) - No Representative gov't allowed (it is like slavery) - *Executive* operations can be run by a separate *Aristocracy* - Small countries may(?) see some value to it; but forms can vary with size
Scriptural Consistency of Scholarship (Christian Worldview)	Most consistent	Somewhat consistent	Inconsistent (its ideas influenced Communism)

An illustration of Locke's vision and structure of good society might look something like this diagram below (his view is introductory and incomplete, as will be seen). In studying this diagram, however, notice how Locke alludes to other institutions in society besides a collection of individuals and the government they have chosen, and that is a vital connection point to the next chapter:[55]

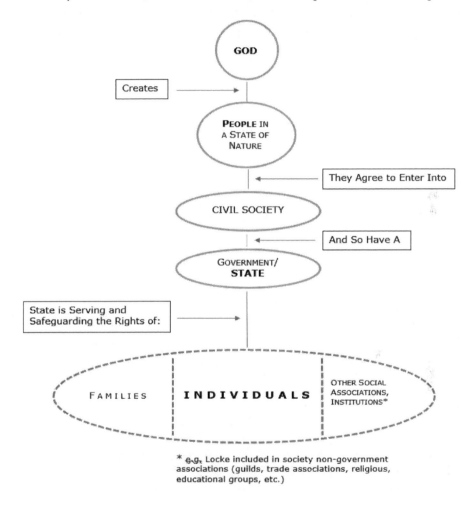

Fig 6.1. Social Structure Under a Social Contract (Locke's)   © 2018 P. Talbot

---

[55] *See* J. Budziszewski, Written on the Heart: The Case for Natural Law 112 (1997).

DISCUSSION QUESTIONS:

1. Of the varying SK theories, which do you think most accurately depicts human nature? Is Hobbes right or Locke on the State of Nature (refer to the Table above)?

2. Do you agree that Locke's SK theory is most consistent with biblical views on society? Is consent of the governed a biblical idea, a good idea?

3. Is there a connection between the idea God is the source of government (in Chapter 5) and the idea of having a SK in forming a government? If so, what is that connection? (Is one perhaps the source of government (God) and the other an ideal for its implementation (SK) – i.e., the best *"how"* in starting it)?

PRAYER POINTS:

1. Pray that you would have integrity and understand your role as a citizen in civil society and its government.
2. Pray for societies that are run by ungodly leaders, where the voices of the just and the poor are often silenced or ignored.
3. Pray for just and godly government in your country and everywhere.

CHAPTER 7

SPHERE SOVEREIGNTY

Write these things on the door frames of your house,
teach them to your children.
(Deuteronomy 6:9)

~The fundamental building block of a good society is the family, along
with other institutions; it is not the State.~

Introduction

Another more sophisticated design for social structuring than a simpler SK
theory like Locke's above, is something called Sphere Sovereignty (SS). It is not
inconsistent with Locke's SK views, including his idea of consensual government, and SS can even incorporate (or subsume) SK ideas, but is far richer and
expands upon it. Although SS has earlier traces in history, its greatest development came through Abraham Kuyper (1837 - 1920), a Dutch Christian, scholar,
statesman, and philosopher. In SS, Kuyper offers a divine design for a healthy
society.[56] It is the strongest Christian model I have seen, and I commend it to
your study.[57]

---

[56] For a short introduction, see Dean Jesse, *Introducing Kuyper's "Sphere Sovereignty,"*
EMERGING SCHOLARS BLOG, InterVarsity's Emerging Scholars Network (Sept. 26, 2014),
https://blog.emergingscholars.org/2014/09/sphere-sovereignty/.

[57] Another incomplete or over-simplified, but not necessarily incorrect view of society
is Luther's. He saw humanity divided into two kingdoms, the earthly one, comprised of
believers and unbelievers, and the heavenly one comprised of believers only. The first is
governed by the civil magistrate/State (most of whom he assumed would be Christians),
the second by the clergy/Church. Luther also saw three hierarchies, the family, Church,

According to Kuyper, God's design for a healthy society involves much more than the State (civil government) and individuals and their families. The State is only one institution in society among equal institutions, or *spheres* in society, such as the Church (religious institutions), family, business associations, educational institutions, and arts. The individual is still an important member of society and can have his/her own sphere. Each sphere has jurisdiction or domain over certain subject matters in society. That's why it's called, *sphere sovereignty* (SS).

Can you identify what each sphere in society should do? An illustration of SS in a healthy society is shown below. Compare it to the illustration of Locke's SK social structure. What do you see is similar and different in the two illustrations (Figs. 6.1 vs. 7.1)?

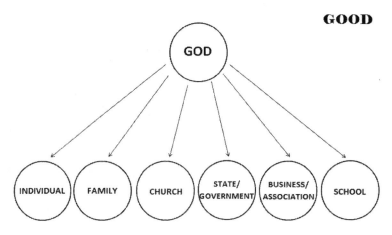

Fig. 7.1

In this diagram, notice how each sphere is of equal dignity and proportion to the others (no hierarchy of superior, controlling institutions). In SS, this is a key element envisioned to provide a system of checks and balances, to prevent any

---

and State, in which the family was seen as the fundamental social unit, supporting Church and State (Eidsmoe, J.A. notes with author). Study Augustine, who influenced Luther and many others on this idea. See JOHN WITTE JR., CHRISTIANITY AND LAW, AN INTRODUCTION 18-19 (John Witte Jr. and Frank Alexander eds., 2006); EIDSMOE, *supra* note 51 at 10-11, 15.

one sphere (usually the State) from dominating the others in a healthy society (see a discussion of this problem and the conflicts it creates in the sections below).[58]

Sphere Cooperation and Sphere Conflicts
Sometimes an overlap on social issues is inevitable, requiring collaboration among the spheres on an issue (e.g., marriage involves inputs from each the family, Church, and even the State, and of course the individuals involved). Sometimes this overlap leads to strong social conflicts as spheres fight over who has authority over an issue, especially when they have very different viewpoints.

In theory, no sphere should intrude upon the chief jurisdictional activities of another sphere. In reality, many conflicts on social issues exist and can be traced back to the simple failure of some institutions to respect the domain and boundaries of other institutions. See the exercise in Discussion Question 3, at the end of this chapter, aimed at helping you sort through some of these issues.

When Things Go Wrong in Some Countries: Sphere Invasions
In some unstable societies, things can get worse than just having jurisdictional turf wars among spheres and social clashes on issues. If any one sphere intrudes upon and begins to take control over another sphere(s), society can get quickly out of whack. If the Church overtakes the other spheres, we have a religious tyranny or dictatorship. Consider times when the Roman Catholic Church had an army; Protestants too, including some Calvinists, have exhibited similar tendencies.

If a family rules everything, including the entire State apparatus, we have a dynasty – usually some sort of monarchy (some are good and most are not); this usually results in an increase in graft, infighting, and loss of meritocracy. If the business sector controls the State, that is probably indicative of widespread bribery and corruption, and undue influence in shaping State laws.

Historically, however it is most typically the State, having the greatest coercive power and influence of all the spheres, which encroaches upon and can

---

[58] Each institutional, non-State sphere is considered an *intermediary institution*, serving to prevent the State from exercising tyranny over its citizens. Each has its own inherent value and purpose in a just society also.

swallow up entire institutions. In common vernacular, this can manifest into the bad historical examples of *Socialism* or *Communism* (depicted below), along with other statist-totalitarian kinds of regimes.[59]

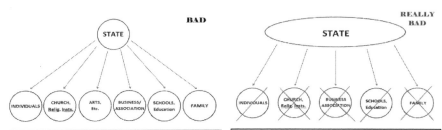

In Socialism, we see the State dominating social institutions. It runs the economy. Church, family, and education may all still exist (in European, Democratic Socialism, not in Communist Socialism), but business is highly regulated (profit re-distributed); high levels of tax and government spending to solve social ills. Restrictions on income and free enterprise.

Fig. 7.2   © 2015 P Talbot

In this diagram of Communism, Xs signify virtual sphere elimination; single slashes /, indicate State control or redefinition. Controls can vary in Communism. The State runs the economy, breaks up the family, eliminates the Church, educates individuals (if at all) as economic units. Loss of liberty. Supposed to eventually eliminate State, but it never happens.

Fig. 7.3   © 2015 P Talbot

Notice how in the diagrams above the balance and equality of the spheres has been lost, with the State assuming the controlling role; in some ideologies, it takes the place of God, and seeks to orchestrate all social functions (with its coercive power whenever necessary).

It is interesting to test your own political inclinations, and see if you should make some adjustments: How you identify politically is related to where you would insert the State in these diagrams. If you would put the State at the center and above all other social institutions, or consider the other spheres not impor- tant, you are likely a leftist, Socialist, or Communist. If you put the State in line with other spheres (not elevating it, same level), you are likely a Libertarian or Conservative (in the U.S. sense). If a theist, you honor God as Sovereign over society, and see the State as subject to Him, and that is correct. Some Socialists are theists and would insert a circle for God above the State (some Scandinavian countries seek this), but this still gives too much authority and credit to the State.

---

[59] Such as *Fascism* and *Nazism* (see Chapter 10 below on government forms). Consider Nazi State influence in German Christian churches in the events surrounding WWII.

Sphere Connections to Law, Justice, and Government

In a good, healthy society (Fig. 7.1), consider how law, government (authority of some kind), and justice should exist **in each sphere**. The State, or civil government, is not the only one providing law, government, and justice in society, other spheres are included too. Sure, the State plays an important role. It even makes laws for some of the other spheres, as well as regulating rights or activities, and even tensions between them. But the State is not the only player in a healthy society. Other spheres maintain their own authorities and legal systems, of sorts. Identify what sorts of authorities and "laws" (rules) exist in other spheres, and what sort of justice is to be found there. Consider families (curfew and dating rules), churches (ecclesiastical and membership rules), educational institutions (academic standards, rules of trustees) and business enterprises (articles of incorporation, and by-laws) as just some examples. Even the individual has self-governance (how you govern yourself).

All the spheres even have dispute resolution procedures that may not involve the civil courts (i.e., mom and dad, in the case of a family), and in other institutions, even churches, things like boards of review, disciplinary panels, and dispute review panels, among other mechanisms. In short, in each sphere we see law (rules) regulating conduct, plus enforcement systems, and governing authority, hopefully implementing justice. It's a fascinating system in which government and justice are held by more than just the State, as each sphere does its part and is allowed to rule in its subject-area jurisdiction.

Subsidiarity, A Similar Catholic Model

A Catholic version similar to Sphere Sovereignty is called *Subsidiarity*. It is more hierarchically arranged, with the Church sitting above the State (not on the same horizontal plane), and other institutions underneath it. The one's higher up are supposed to help the ones below. [60]

Some variations of Kuyper's model, increasing in sophistication, have also surfaced over time (see Herman Dooyeweerd). Kuyper's model remains a strong and valid one in its basic structure, today.

---

[60] *See* Kent A. Van Til, *Subsidiarity and Sphere Sovereignty: A Match Made In . . . ?*, 69 THEOLOGICAL STUDIES 610 (2008) (comparing similarities and differences between SS and Subsidiarity, and noting some growing convergence among scholars in the two ideas).

DISCUSSION QUESTIONS and EXERCISE:

1. What roles and activities in society are ascribed to each sphere? That is, what is the jurisdiction of each sphere?

2. Which sphere(s) is/are primarily responsible for the economic welfare and growth in society? (If you say it's the State, I hope you think again.)

3. How does Sphere Sovereignty (SS) apply to the following issues or situations? Specifically, in which of the examples below do you see violations of SS principles? In which sphere(s) should the issues or situations listed below be decided (i.e., which sphere(s) should exercise jurisdiction over these matters)? Should any illustrations below involve cooperation between spheres (which ones and how much cooperation); any risks in doing that?:

    a) State owned enterprises;
    b) Building roads and infrastructure in a community (or a country), including its ports, airports, and mass rapid-transit systems (subways, busses, etc.);
    c) Developing waste management systems (garbage collection, sewage, etc.);
    d) State-run healthcare systems; i.e., who should run health care in a community or a country: the State, private entities, or some combination of each? Does the size of a nation's population make a difference? Consider examples seeming to function somewhat smoothly (in the U.K., possibly?) to something like the Affordable Care Act (a/k/a "Obama Care") in the USA, in which an estimated six million people *lost* their health insurance due to compulsory participation

and increased costs imposed on the U.S. middle class, to subsidize the program (the fate of that Act remains uncertain, and is in a steady state of constitutional challenge, at the time of this writing);

e) Higher education (university levels), funding it and to what level?;

f) In some public schools in the West, mandating sex education of children in elementary school, often with graphic sexual content, taught against the wishes of parents, and now also including mandatory classes to indoctrinate children to support homosexual and transgender sexual identities;

g) Government welfare programs including education and job skills training, which may inhibit or compete against those offered by charities and faith-based institutions;

h) Prohibiting a church or other place of worship from starting an elementary school on its grounds;

i) Arresting parents in Sweden and Germany for homeschooling, and separating children from their parents for doing so (several real cases);

j) Taking people's property to build a shopping center (also a real case);

k) Deciding how many children you can have (what if a religious leader or State official tells you how many children you can have; is that alright?);

l) Deciding how much money you can have, or can keep;

m) Determining who you can marry, including if it's allowed to be the same sex, or many partners;

n) Deciding what you and your children should believe about life, God, and other big questions in life?

4. How might an understanding of SS help explain either right-leaning or left-leaning political ideologies that people seem to have?

5. Are law, government, and authority of some kind operating in each sphere (i.e., besides law in the State sphere)? If so, can you identify some examples of this happening? How, if at all, do the operations of such

things in these spheres help decentralize power, or shift it away, from the State?

6. How might honoring SS in society improve justice?

7. Are all spheres in all societies operating at all times; or do some institutions emerge at various stages, as societies develop and grow over time? If the latter, is that situation alright; is it something to be expected?

PRAYER POINTS:

1. Pray that you would have the wisdom of Solomon, specifically in seeing how many social conflicts are based on misunderstandings of the distinct jurisdictions of different institutions (spheres) in society.
2. Pray that you would be a godly example to your family and friends and exhibit the fruits of the Spirit, especially in conflicting social issues.
3. Pray for peace and civil dialogue in your country on controversial issues.

CHAPTER 8

SEPARATION OF CHURCH
AND STATE

*Then he said to them, "So give back to Caesar what is Caesar's, and to
God what is God's."*
(Matthew 22:21)

As YOU NOTICED in the Sphere Sovereignty information above, two of the very important spheres in all of history are Church and State. They often clash in their jurisdictions. The idea of a separation of Church and State is supposed to mean the institutions of Church and State are separate, but it never meant that religious views of ethics and justice could not influence the morality of laws.[61]

Scriptures Shaping Values and Laws in Society Isn't a Violation of Separation of Church and State

All law reflects some kind of underlying moral values and is shaped by ethical standards in defining justice. This is so because laws tell us how to live and conduct our affairs and how to treat each other in society. Law is normative. The idea that laws can only be secular (*Secularism* is an ideology), and that this is somehow a "neutral" approach to lawmaking, is a myth. *Secularism* is itself a religious view of sorts,

---

[61] Religious laws regulating ceremonial, ritual and worship practices are a different issue. These are not usually appropriate for inculcation into general civil law in society, but Scripture's standards for human ethics, like the last five of the Ten Commandments, should be allowed, especially as indicating God's truth and wisdom (*see infra Fig. 8.1.*). See EIDSMOE, *supra* note 51, at 19-24 (examining intended meaning of separation under the First Amendment, U.S. Constitution, and its recent distortions).

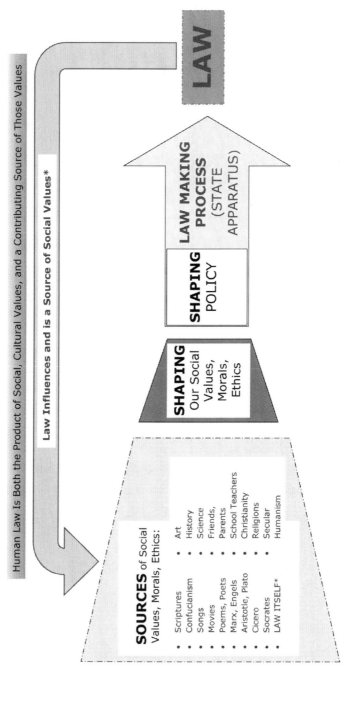

Fig. 8.1 Religious Values and Ethics Contributing to the Lawmaking Process.   © 2018 P. Talbot

Human Law Is Both the Product of Social, Cultural Values, and a Contributing Source of Those Values

Law Influences and is a Source of Social Values*

LAW

LAW MAKING PROCESS (STATE APPARATUS)

SHAPING POLICY

SHAPING Our Social Values, Morals, Ethics

SOURCES of Social Values, Morals, Ethics:

- Scriptures
- Confucianism
- Songs
- Movies
- Poems, Poets
- Marx, Engels
- Aristotle, Plato
- Cicero
- Socrates
- LAW ITSELF*

- Art
- History
- Science
- Friends,
- Parents
- School Teachers
- Christianity
- Religions
- Secular
- Humanism

embodying its own set of values and claims about Ultimate Reality, that could go into shaping law, just like any other system of ethics influencing law. Secularism is a view; it is not neutral. Secularized efforts to strip superior ethical standards sourced in historical religions is simply unacceptable, and biased viewpoint discrimination. It is not just. See how it should work in this diagram (Fig. 8.1).

As the illustration shows, values from all sorts of sources might go into shaping a nation's laws. It's inevitable. In fact, whoever controls the values in society (the culture) is likely to control law. It makes no sense to allow inclusion or consideration of values-shaping ideas from great literature, the arts, music, ancient Greek and Roman philosophy, history, Confucianism, secularism, Marxism (in Venezuela, and elsewhere), Hollywood, social media pundits, and what our parents or teachers taught us, in shaping our values for laws, and then seeking to eliminate Scriptural values from consideration. In lawmaking, this is especially improper when Scripture's values are superior, as indicative of God's will.

I have discussed above (in Scriptural jurisprudence) the ways in which Scripture can shape values, and thus laws in a society, as it has done historically.

Should Christians Serve in Government? (Yes)

Some say Christians should not get involved in politics or government, either because it violates the separation of Church and State, or is a corrupt (dirty) business. Both suggestions are incorrect. Government is a godly thing (see above) and its corruption by sin is a call for Christians to get involved. In constitutional, democratic republics (from the USA to Indonesia, Singapore, Australia, and in most democracies in the world), Christians are required to get involved in their governments as a means of submitting to it, and some are called to full-time service in it. Christians must be salt and light in all fields of life, including in the administration of law, justice and government (see Matthew. 5:13-16).

In *Politics According to the Bible*, author Wayne Grudem supports the idea of *Significant Christian Influence on Government*.[62] This idea basically reflects the ideas on Christian influence indicated above and throughout this Study Guide (consider biblical examples showing this influence, including, Daniel influencing

---

[62] WAYNE GRUDEM, POLITICS ACCORDING TO THE BIBLE, A COMPREHENSIVE RESOURCE FOR UNDERSTANDING MODERN POLITICAL ISSUES IN LIGHT OF SCRIPTURE 55-76 (2010).

Nebuchadnezzar, Samuel influencing Saul, and John the Baptist rebuking Herod).

Five Incorrect Views on Christians Serving in Government

In contrast to the correct view, Grudem identifies five erroneous views and misconceptions on Christians' role in government, including that they should just not get involved in it at all:[63]

(a) *Government should compel religion* (meaning religious worship practices of one particular religion; he cites the Thirty Years' War (1618-1648) and similar wars among Christian denominations in Europe as typifying this incorrect view).[64]

(b) *Government should exclude religion* (this is the dominant, secularist view in America today, preached by its media, educational, and entertainment elites; I have addressed its falsity and bigotry above).[65]

(c) *All [civil] government is evil and demonic* (some church pastors notoriously favor this wrong view; calling politics *dirty*, and are the first to decry Christians' involvement in it; adherents of this view tend to be extreme pacifists, and that is very unhealthy, as Scripture (OT/NT) doesn't actually teach this).[66]

(d) *Christians should do evangelism, not politics* (this view appreciates the importance of internal transformation of people in society and God's kingdom, but it ignores God's design and call for godly, ethical government, civic duty, and His call to justice).[67]

(e) *Christians should do politics, not evangelism* (this is the Social Gospel view of the late nineteenth century, admirable for addressing many social ills, but

---

[63] *Id.* at 23-54.

[64] *Id.* at 23-29.

[65] *Id.* at 29-36.

[66] *Id.* at 38-42 (Jesus' teaching about turning the other cheek is about responding to personal insults, for His disciples; it's not a prescription for national policy or self-defense).

[67] *Id.* at 44-53.

sadly ignoring the internal, life changing power of the Gospel of Jesus Christ).[68]

In short, Christians indeed have a duty of involvement in civil affairs, as should all citizens of the State, as indicated in its constitution. To shun this role violates Romans 13 to submit to the civil authorities; it is shirking the civil duties called for in that kind of government. Some Christians are called directly to serve in government, but all should be involved in the affairs of their State.

A short essay illustrating various, historical Christian perspectives on the separation of Church and State, according to different denominations, is available in Appendix VII, Link 8.1.

DISCUSSION QUESTIONS:

1. What is the intended meaning behind the idea of separation of Church and State? Is it a good thing or a bad thing (doesn't that depend on what one means by separation)?

2. Should Christians' views on law and public policy be excluded in society from consideration? Does such input violate the idea of an institutional "separation of Church and State?"

3. To what extent should a Christian participate in politics or government? Is *law* a field related to government, or is it separate from that? If related, how might that support an argument that Christian lawyers should also be involved in State, civil government?

---

[68] *Id.* at 53-54. It is not as common a view as it once was. Christians can seek both.

4. Political discourse can often get heavy and antagonistic, especially when opposing viewpoints clash. As Christians, how can we present our views in public discourse, without compromising truth, and without losing our Christian love for those who disagree with us?

PRAYER POINTS:

1. Pray that God would reveal your spiritual gifts to serve your church and community, and your State.
2. Pray for the leaders in your church and their families to get involved in civic social issues, specifically to promote justice.
3. Pray for your local political leaders.
4. Pray that God would grant you wisdom and understanding in dealing with circumstances of opposing viewpoints, and in addressing misconceptions about Christians' involvement in government and policy issues, and in making good laws that advance justice.

CHAPTER 9

SCRIPTURE AND THE BEST FORM(S) OF GOVERNMENT

The heart is deceitful above all things and beyond cure.
Who can understand it?
(Jeremiah 17:9)

SCRIPTURE DOES NOT directly announce which form of government is best. But Scripture and historical experience can suggest some good answers.

Common General Forms

Although **monarchy** (kings, queens, or single rulers)[69] is the most common form seen in ancient and biblical history (OT), and even though God allowed it in ancient Israel, and even though Jesus is King of Kings and reigns in an eternal kingdom in which we are His subjects and help spread that kingdom, that does not necessarily make it the best option at a human level, since we are all sinners (Romans 3:23).

In looking at the ancient biblical account and history (OT and other sources), and seeing the sheer volume (prevalence) of kings ruling nations and cities in the ancient world, coupled with God's clear instructions in OT Scripture that He

---

[69] The term "king" in ancient and OT literature is used to mean more than the ruler of a nation; it is also used for lesser rulers (of cities, etc.) and magistrates, suggesting it is not a consistent, single kind of government to start with. *See* ChristianAnswers.net, *Who are the . . . kings in the Bible*, The Bible Encyclopedia, https://christiananswers.net/dictionary/king.html (last visited 26 April 2019) (listing kings in Israel, and foreign kings noted in the Bible).

was intentionally choosing certain individuals to rule as *kings*, it's hard to imagine God had any other form of government in mind than monarchy.[70] However, Scripture (NT especially), and lessons drawn from history in the Church era, teach us additional principles about sinful human nature that suggest better alternative forms of government than monarchy.

Gradually, throughout history in the Church era, serious thinkers began to see the risks in kingship, and seizing on such additional principles in Scripture, started to strongly urge more representative ideas of government. This culminated in some Reformers (Calvin and others), who saw *individual* salvations as important (to secure one's eternity), but then also translated that individualistic emphasis into concerns for individual rights and individuals having a voice in government (ideas that Locke of course espoused). This shift helped establish America's *democratic republic* and has inspired subsequent democratic governments around the world.[71]

First, it should be noted when Israel demanded having a king (like the other nations of the ancient world, so it could wage war like them), God saw this as an act of rebellion, a rejection of Him as king (1 Samuel 8:7, 12:17).[72] But God accommodated the Israelites' request due to their stubbornness. Second, when Israel started having its kings, including in the divided kingdoms of Israel and Judah, the results were largely disastrous.[73] Most of Israel's kings were idolatrous and led the people into corruption and sin, invoking God's wrath (even

---

[70] Historically, this had led many to incorrectly assert something called a *divine right of kings* (as if the king is God's infallible viceroy on earth). *See* PARKER, *supra* note 54 (explaining Locke's severe and accurate criticisms of Richard Filmer's reading of Genesis to support a so-called *divine right of king*s).

[71] This summary is simplistic (necessarily so), yet is not intended to disregard some efforts in ancient history toward more democratic governments (i.e., in Greece and Rome). Importantly, in sharp contrast to kingships in the ancient world, very few countries today have a king (or monarch). Most countries claim to be democracies of some kind, while any remaining kings or monarchs in the world usually have very limited powers (with some exceptions).

[72] Not because of an inherent evil in kingship, but because of God's covenant with Israel. *See* THE NIV STUDY BIBLE, text note. 1 *Samuel.* 8:7 (Zondervan 2011) (suggesting this); but see sections below on inherent difficulties with kingship.

[73] *See* 1, 2 *Kings* (citing numerous examples).

if they started well). Only a handful, mostly in Judah, served with justice and honored God.[74] Israel's experience with kings shines a light on the sinful nature of humans, and suggests a lesser concentration of power in a single ruler is best (something with checks and balances).

Another serious issue with monarchy is the virtual impossibility of a single ruler reigning with real competence over a very large nation (i.e., a valid practical concern). Such a difficulty makes it quite uncommon to find **pure (absolute) monarchies** (or at least many successful ones), in the first place.[75] Instead, monarchies tend to morph into various versions of power sharing arrangements, like **oligarchies** (a group of elite leaders), or will include councils of advisors and similar bodies to assist rulers, or may simply shrink in power through intentional constitutions and laws.[76] In short, successful and good *absolute monarchies* seldom exist.

As to Scriptural insights, the Bible clearly states and shows all humans are sinners (see Romans 3:23, and similar Scriptures about Israel, and its kings). Consequently, kings easily become bad rulers, especially if given too much power. History shows us many examples.[77] While Jesus (God) is himself a king and will rule as such eternally, he is not limited by our sinful shortcomings. He will always be a good king. Scripture therefore shows that governing through powerful elites or kings, as sinners, is not a good idea. Systems with checks on power and control are better systems against sin.

---

[74] *Id.*

[75] *See Definitions for Absolute Monarchy,* DEFINITIONS, https://www.definitions.net/definition/absolute+monarchy (last visited 26 April 2019).

[76] A constitutional monarchy is better than an absolute one because it limits a monarch's power by laws. *See Define Absolute Rule,* STUDY.COM, https://study.com/academy/answer/define-absolute-rule.html (last visited 26 April 2019) (distinguishing absolute and constitutional monarchy; note, this site links to several short and interesting videos for students). *See Definition of Oligarchy,* COLLINS ENGLISH DICTIONARY, https://www.collinsdictionary.com/dictionary/english/oligarchy (last visited 26 April 2019).

[77] This has led many to agree with Lord Acton's famous saying, "Absolute power corrupts absolutely." *See* Gary Martin, THE PHRASE FINDER, https://www.phrases.org.uk/meanings/absolute-power-corrupts-absolutely.html (last visited 26 April 2019) (explaining the saying's history).

Accordingly, a suggested form of government providing such checks and balances, to the greatest degree known so far in history, is a **constitutional republic**. Sometimes it is also called a *democratic republic*, or *constitutional democracy*, or more summarily, a **constitutional democratic republic**.[78] This is a representative form of government (a *republic*), in which the entire population does not rule itself and issue all laws directly (as it would in a so-called **pure democracy**). Instead they choose qualified representatives to govern in a system of checks and balances, with power sharing, as set out in a constitution (that is why it is more Scripturally compatible). Often it is typified by having three branches of government (*legislative, executive,* and *judicial* branches).[79] It is a system also useable in all levels of civil government.

Summary and Cautions on Forms

I emphasize this is a *good form* of government for a relatively *good people*, operating under a *good and just constitution* (i.e., one seeking to safeguard God-given human rights and liberties). It makes no sense to have this *form* of government under a constitution whose *substance* fails to cherish these God-given rights and liberties, or whose *leaders* lack a true commitment to honor it.[80]

In this world, no government system is going to be completely successful. That will only come after Jesus finally establishes his kingdom, one without sin (Isaiah 35:8-9; Revelation 21:27). But an ideal form in the interim, so far as human history and knowledge can illuminate us, is having a good constitutional democratic republic. That's because it optimizes a system of checks and balance against our sinful human natures (if it also incorporates the other conditions stated above).[81]

---

[78] *See* FRANCIS J. BECKWITH, POLITICS FOR CHRISTIANS, STATECRAFT AS SOULCRAFT 60-63 (2010) (calling it a *Liberal Constitutional Democracy*: liberal in the classical sense of signifying the protection of liberties and freedoms, not Socialist). Some also use the term *Representative Democracy* to distinguish it from a *pure democracy* (majority rule). *See id.*

[79] *See* U.S. CONST. arts. I, II, III (inspiring similar examples worldwide).

[80] Reminiscent of the common adage in many law schools to *avoid form over substance; cf.* 2 *Tim.* 3:5 (*having a form of godliness but denying its power . . .*).

[81] In America, this form has served well, for a long time, under a good and just constitution, so long as its people have sought justice. It has survived the scourge of slavery (an area

Ideologies and the Political Spectrum

In short, there are many isms and ideologies out there in the world, historically and now, and this can cause students to get very confused about them, including those dealing with economic systems that governments are supposed to manage (see next chapter addressing such economic systems). So we hear of: *Fascism, Nazism, Totalitarianism* (Dictatorships), *Socialism, Communism, Capitalism, Constitutionalism,* and so forth. One of the reasons this can seem so confusing is because of a *political spectrum* that scholars have sometimes come up with, which as classically drawn, is incorrect. Fig. 9.1 shows this common but incorrect spectrum.[82]

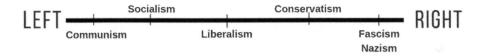

Fig. 9.1 Inaccurate but well known spectrum

A more accurate political spectrum is this:

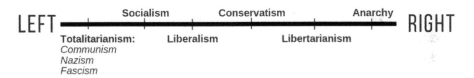

Fig. 9.2 Corrected spectrum

Fascism, Nazism, Socialism, and Communism actually have more in common than students first see, because they each lead to tyrannical dictatorships. Fascism starts out with strong leadership preserving business classes, elites and their interests, before suppressing them; while Socialism fights class systems at

---

and era of injustice), and a civil war that eradicated it. Traditional American values have been sliding for decades, however, and its future is to be seen.

[82] Both the incorrect and correct depictions of the political spectrum above, come from EIDSMOE, *supra* note 51, at 79-80.

first, but both isms result in eventual loss of freedom by political elites and dictators, and they end with the same suffering in society.[83]

An important video is provided below (see note 84), which gives a very clear explanation of the real political spectrum, and discusses key distinctions between monarchy, anarchy, oligarchy, democracy, and a constitutional republic, in graphic color and style; although discussing this in the American context, the truths in this video are globally solid and valuable.[84] You will need to review this video to answer questions below, so study it carefully.[85]

DISCUSSION QUESTIONS:

1. After seeing the video above, what did you like about it? How does it help you keep these concepts straight?

2. How might the information in this video apply to issues in your own country?

3. How is Jesus different than earthly kings, and how is his kingdom different?

4. Why does a system of checks and balances and representative government, as in a constitutional republic, seem to work better than other kinds of government seen in history?

---

[83] *Id.*

[84] *RCO64, The American form of government,* YouTube (Aug. 27, 2013), https://www.youtube.com/watch?v=VogzExP3qhI.

[85] One shortcoming, or clarification: The video says Communism results in a strong State (statism). Communism actually seeks to eventually abolish the State, but it has never succeeded in doing so, and has always ended up in a State-controlled society.

5. For more information about human nature, and how assumptions about that inevitably affect our choices about the optimal forms of government, see JEFFREY A. BRAUCH, FLAWED PERFECTION (2017) (studying social issues and institutions in light of human nature).

PRAYER POINTS:

1. Pray that you would understand in a new way how God's Word is living and active, sharper than any double-edged sword, including seeing its guidance on good government.
2. Pray for greater wisdom and understanding of God's Kingdom in contrast to earthly kingdoms.
3. Pray for national leaders, lawmakers, and governing rulers not to fall into the traps of Satan's lies about human nature, and the best form of government.

CHAPTER 10

SCRIPTURE AND BEST SOCIO-ECONOMIC STATE ARRANGEMENTS

The LORD detests dishonest scales, but accurate weights
find favor with him.
(Proverbs 11:1)

That each of them may eat and drink, and find satisfaction in all their
toil—this is the gift of God.
(Ecclesiastes 3:12)

THIS CHAPTER CONTINUES with the subject of isms and ideologies introduced in Chapter 9. Sometimes the ordering of society involves a specific economic structuring within a particular government system. I mentioned already three of the most common economic-government systems and arrangements today: Communism, Socialism and Capitalism. This chapter asks, which of these is best?

Communism
Classic Marxism involves the violent overthrow of an economic class of people (capitalists, industrial elites, the *bourgeoise*), in order to eventually achieve a hypothetical stateless and classless society in which all property rights are abolished,

and everyone would have the same amount of wealth in society.[86] Initially, the revolutionaries were to be industrial workers, the *proletariat*. Actually, in countries like the former U.S.S.R, China, and later in South America, revolutions were run more by peasant farmers and instigating intellectual elites (i.e., Lenin in Russia).[87] The revolution was supposed to establish a *democratic, dictatorship of the proletariat* (Socialist State), steering eventually toward a classless society, Communism; it was to spread internationally.[88] Socialism, accordingly, was considered a vital intermediate stage between Capitalism and Communism.[89]

Communism is also atheistic.[90] It has never worked and never will. The ideology has never gotten past its bloody Socialist revolutions, and impoverished State-run economy stages, in any country. It has been an utter failure economically, and is horrific in its care of people, as the leaders of this ideology have been responsible for about 100 million deaths, internationally, in the 20th Century.[91]

This table estimates the number of deaths by country caused by Communism in the last century.[92]

---

[86] *See* Terrence Ball & Richard Dagger *Communism*, ENCYCLOPEDIA BRITANNICA (June 26, 2017), https://www.britannica.com/topic/communism (historical overview; however, note the authors' reference to historical examples of Christians sharing property and living in communities as a kind of *Communism*, is incorrect, in this author's view).

[87] *Id.* Lenin said revolution should start in non-industrial, agrarian countries, to cast off Western imperialism, and required a *vanguard party* of intellectuals to lead it. *Id.*

[88] *Id.* Stalin altered this, urging *Socialism in one country* (Russia), above all else. *Id.*

[89] *Id.* In classic Marxism, two stages (and revolutions) were assumed: (1) a *capitalist* one, (2) followed by the *proletariat* one, with a Socialist stage, before evolving into Communism. After Lenin died (1924), Leon Trotsky sought instead a single, permanent revolution (not two-stages), still very anti-capitalist-imperialist, and decidedly international. Stalin came into power, however, and disagreeing sharply with Trotsky's ideas, had him exiled to Mexico and assassinated him there in 1940. *Id.*

[90] *Id.*; *see also* Kate T. et. al., *Communism vs Socialism*, DIFFEN LLC, http://www.diffen.com/difference/Communism_vs_Socialism (last visited 29 April 2019)

[91] *See* David Floyd, *What is the Difference Between Communism and Socialism?*, INVESTOPEDIA, https://www.investopedia.com/ask/answers/100214/what-difference-between-communism-and-socialism.asp (Jan. 5, 2018 12:45 EST) (noting historic atrocities); Ball & Dagger, *supra* note 86 (failures of the *Great Leap Forward* in China).

[92] WAYNE GRUDEM & BARRY ASMUS, THE POVERTY OF NATIONS: A SUSTAINABLE SOLUTION 125 (2009) (citing JAY W. RICHARDS, MONEY, GREED, AND GOD: WHY CAPITALISM IS THE SOLUTION AND NOT THE PROBLEM 11-19 (2009) (internal citations omitted)).

Country	Number of People killed under communist regimes
China	65 Million
U.S.S.R.	20 Million
North Korea	2 Million
Cambodia	2 Million
African nations	1.7 Million
Afghanistan	1.5 Million
Vietnam	1 Million
Eastern European nations	1 Million
Latin American nations	150, 000
The international communist movement	About 10, 000

Table 10.1 International Communist deaths by nations

Communist intellectuals had their ideas shaped as students. So here is a caution: *any ideology that teaches human lives should be sacrificed to achieve utopia for the rest of society is one you should avoid, stand against, and challenge.*

A summary statement for Communism is: ***from each according to his ability, to each according to his need.***[93] This means no matter how skilled and creative someone is at producing goods and wealth, whatever s/he accumulates or achieves above a given arbitrary line, set by the State, can't be kept and shared as s/he wishes; it is taken from them and given to others who have less, to create sameness of income. It is a complete disincentive to ingenuity, innovation, and effort, steering people away from these, to doing only the bare minimum of work (after all, why work for anything above a set line if you can't keep it?).

Socialism

This is sometimes used interchangeably with Communism, but specifically refers to that intermediate stage between Capitalism and Communism (noted above). It is considered more an economic ordering than a political one in society, but is obviously connected to political ideologies (as Communism is). Socialism basically refers to a *State-run economy.*[94] It can allow for private property and earnings,

---

[93] Kate T., *supra* note 90.

[94] Floyd, *supra* note 91. In Socialism, the main means of production, distribution, and exchange are owned by the State; in Communism, by *all in common*; and in Capitalism, by

but it controls the distribution of surpluses (profits).[95] Socialism sees the State as the chief benefactor (provider) of social welfare, requiring high taxation and spending, including subsidies in things like education, health care, child care, and infrastructure, but giving little room for the private sector's involvement in these. It necessarily involves restrictions on individual freedoms and private property, without completely eliminating them. It can be theistic (seldom) or atheistic.[96]

Socialism is a broad term, and can exist on a spectrum from very strict State control (Communist Socialism), to combinations with Capitalism in some Western democratic societies, creating mixed economies. (e.g., in some of the Americas, Europe-Scandinavian countries, and Australia).[97]

A summary statement for Socialism is: *from each according to his ability, to each according to his contribution [State-alleged value of his/her work].* [98]

Capitalism

This is basically the idea of a *free market economy* (in theory). It may require *State-regulation* of business and commercial enterprise, but not *State-running* of the economy. It can work in a couple of different political systems, but is most suitable with democratic republics because free markets require individual autonomy, creativity (entrepreneurship), freedom of association, and honoring of property (i.e., private property is expected), and other basic human rights.

Some shortcomings of capitalism are the tendency toward greed and selfishness in some less scrupulous corporations and businesses (including sometimes taking advantage of labor/employees), and being prone to economic collusion

---

private interests. Id.; see also Kate T., *supra* note 90; Ball & Dagger, *supra* note 86.

[95] Kate T., *supra* note 90.

[96] *Id.*

[97] *Id.; see* Floyd, *supra* note 91. States may combine words like Democratic or Republic with Socialism to define their ideological character. Actually, this is very unhelpful in describing a State as either more Communist-totalitarian, or open and Democratic. Communist North Korea is called the People's Democratic Republic of Korea. It actually has no democracy or freedom. China is called the People's Republic of China, but is still a Communist State. Cuba is similarly misnamed the Republic of Cuba. *See generally id.*

[98] Kate T., *supra* note 90.

and anti-competitive behavior (e.g., oligopolies, monopolies, and anti-trust violations). Some of the latter activities actually distort markets (prices), impede healthy competition, and hurt consumers. Capitalism works rather justly for all, however, when government keeps a watchful (regulatory) eye on free enterprise, without dominating it (statism).[99]

Recent admirable efforts toward *Corporate Social Responsibility* (CSR), either voluntarily undertaken by corporations, or as part of international guidelines involving agreements among their States, have improved situations in some parts of the world.[100] Significantly, such efforts properly acknowledge the *central role of businesses* (rather than the State), in generating economic growth, and improving individual wealth and general welfare, in their nations.

A saying for Capitalism is: ***from each according to his ability to each according to what s/he has earned.***[101]

Summary Diagram, Socio-Economic Systems

The following somewhat humorous diagram helps summarize these economic systems.[102]

---

[99] Failure of such checks in the U.S. has led to serious economic crises, including globally, with the latest being the sub-prime mortgage crisis in 2008-2010, where financial institutions took unreasonable risks and covered it up.

[100] Some of these efforts are serious, and sincere; in other cases they may be examples of lip service or marketing tools. In any case, sincere efforts should be encouraged. *See* Patrick M. Talbot, *Social Responsibility in Corporate Investment*, 8 Dong-A J. Int'l. Bus. Trans. L. 1 (2012) (discussing international systems, and voluntary CSR efforts, sometimes succeeding).

[101] *See* "Illuminati" et.al., *Capitalism vs Socialism*, Diffen LLC, https://www.diffen.com/difference/Capitalism_vs_Socialism (last visited 29 April, 2019). For a high quality, short video summarizing all three systems, see Investopedia, *The Difference Between Communism and Socialism*, https://www.investopedia.com/video/play/difference-between-communism-and-socialism/ (last updated 26 Nov., 2018).

[102] Illustrations by Susanna Talbot (adapted from similar versions of a concept known as *Bovine Economics* in Google Images, http://images.google.com). *State*, in this illustration, again means civil government at any national or local level.

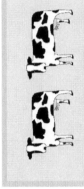

CAPITALISM

You have two cows.
You sell one of them and buy a bull.
They mate and make more cows.
Your herd multiplies, and the economy grows.

SOCIALISM

You have two cows.
The State takes one and gives it to your neighbour.

COMMUNISM

You have two cows.
The State takes both of them and gives you some of the milk.

Fig 10.1 Comparing the three systems

Summary: Isms, Ideologies, and Forms

In sum, the best State-social economic arrangement is likely *a free market system, under rule of law, with appropriate government regulation (not a government-run economy), and which honors basic human and economic rights (is just), while curtailing improper (illegal) activity.* State-private sector shared ventures may also be acceptable in such an arrangement, so long as these honor basic Sphere Sovereignty (SS) principles. The best corresponding form of government, conducive to this system and to general human flourishing, is likely a *Constitutional Democratic Republic*, allowing free enterprise (freedom of association, etc.). This is according to current knowledge, historical experience, and is consistent with Scriptural wisdom.

DISCUSSION QUESTIONS:

1. What are the similarities and differences between Communism, Socialism, and Capitalism?

2. Which form is most in line with biblical principles and why? Which best achieves human flourishing?

3. Should we have entirely free markets or some regulation? How does human greed in capitalist systems factor into your answer?

PRAYER POINTS:

1. Pray to always be thankful for the freedom you have to use your property and pursue your own economic goals. Pray for those in countries that do not have this.

2. Pray that you would avoid greed of all kinds as you enjoy economic freedoms.

3. Pray for corporations and businesses to recognize their role in economic growth and in contributing to the social and economic welfare and social justice, in their communities, in biblical ways. Pray for them to serve in curbing injustices.

CHAPTER 11

LAW AND ECONOMIC DEVELOPMENT (PUTTING IT ALL TOGETHER)

Do not accept a bribe, for a bribe blinds those who see and twists the
words of the innocent.
(Exodus 23:8)

Extortion turns a wise person into a fool, and a bribe corrupts the heart.
(Ecclesiastes 7:7)

A good name is more desirable than great riches; to be esteemed is better
than silver or gold.
(Proverbs 22:1)

When the sentence for a crime is not quickly carried out, people's hearts
are filled with schemes to do wrong.
(Ecclesiastes 8:11)

Righteousness exalts a nation but sin condemns any people.
(Proverbs 14:34)

THIS SECTION DEALS with the role law should have in promoting justice, and contributing to the overall growth and economic welfare of a nation (its flourishing). This is the capstone and culmination of everything written in this booklet so far. In a sense, this chapter seeks to tie things together: If good and just law is implemented in society, in a governing structure and economic system that respects rights and roles of non-state institutions (SS), and among a relatively good (justice seeking) people, that nation should have economic success. It should also enjoy peace, flourishing, and prosperity in other, non-economic ways. This is the reason I have offered this Study Guide in the first place: so that we can aim for improvements and changes in societies toward a higher good. In doing that, we achieve in part the greatest command in Scripture, to love our neighbors as ourselves (Leviticus. 19:18; Matthew 22:39).

A simple illustration that helps us see the big picture of how law improves society is to think of a soccer game. Imagine trying to play soccer without any rules? You can use your hands, cheat, and even injure your opponent to win, but so could your opponent. A society without law (rules) would be something like that. It would be really hard to accomplish anything good. Now, also picture a soccer game with published rules, but no one paying any attention to them, and no competent and fair referee to enforce them either. These illustrations similarly depict scenarios of what many nations struggle with today. It may help to keep these soccer illustrations in mind as you consider the discussion below.

"Justice and Development" (or 'Law and Development' (L and D))

The focus in this chapter is on improving societies in the developing world, through legal systems that achieve justice, but the information here is broadly applicable. This study harkens to a specialized field of law, known as *Law and Development* (that is, law and economic development; or *L and D*, as referred to in this section). The modern field of study in L and D is several decades old, following European reconstruction and the Bretton Woods Agreement after WWII. Since the beginning, it has gone through various fluctuations and corrections. A growing biblical approach in this field is greatly needed. I offer some general, interim observations, and some suggested readings in this summary. To begin with, a new name for this field might be warranted. Instead of calling it Law and Development, a better term would be *Justice and Development*. I have suggested this in the section title, as law can only help improve economic and other development to the extent it achieves actual justice (hence, the earlier chapters in this Study Guide are essential to the whole effort).

Models and Mistakes

A misconception in the earlier days of L and D (i.e., the *Washington Consensus*)[103] led to an inaccurate picture of law being seen as the ultimate ***cause*** of economic development and growth.[104] It would look like this:

Fig.11.1. Incorrect depiction of law being the ultimate cause of economic and social growth.

Scholarship over time suggests law is more a *facilitator* or *accommodator* for economic growth, and that sustainable economic growth happens in a more organic and natural way through other social forces, like entrepreneurship, social and cultural values, relationships, skills and various activities interacting in society.[105] It can be shown like this:

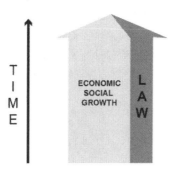

Fig. 11.2. Law comes alongside more naturally occurring economic and social growth, assisting, and facilitating it (the <u>connectedness</u> idea).

---

[103] The Washington Consensus is a fiscally conservative approach that has had some successes, yet perhaps more so in already more economically stable or advanced countries. *See* Katie Willis, Theories And Practices Of Development 56-60 (2d ed. 2011).

[104] The many countries that have lots of law and almost no growth show how this assumption is inaccurate.

[105] Brian Z. Tamanaha, *The Primacy of Society and the Failures of Law and Development*, 44 Cornell Int'l L.J. 209, 214 (2011) (calling this the *connectedness principle of law*; its connection to everything else happening in society, including business, culture, etc.).

In this more accurate model, law *serves* and *comes alongside* economic and social growth, accompanying it, securing it, helping it grow, and sometimes steering it, but is not its chief cause, and not a pure catalyst (although it must lay a foundation; see below). Such growth is *initiated* by other factors in society, rather than by law itself.

Another misconception, in addition to law causing economic growth, is that it did this through a *government-heavy, top-down approach* (a Keynesian view). A better understanding now has led to the idea that development starts at more *grass-roots* levels, in communities having local customs, practices, and some laws, which are either facilitating or hindering that growth.[106]

Some scholars observing these changes in L and D scholarship have abandoned L and D, saying it does not work.[107] But maybe the above approaches and assumptions (like the Washington Consensus being prescribed *in all situations*), is really what does not work, and law still has a vital role to play in development.

Lest we be too hasty to dismiss the impact law has on economic development and welfare, it should be noted the foundational legal system of a nation (i.e., its fundamental laws: its constitution and basic statutes), is very important. Self-critics of L and D lament the only real contributions it has made are in improving *distinct, individual,*[108] *internal legal systems* in a nation (i.e., separate legal fields like contracts, torts, property law, banking law, investment law, criminal law, administrative law, inheritance law, family law, commercial law, tax law, and so on). Contributions and developments in these individual *micro-level* legal systems are indeed very significant for a nation, and it is good to look at ways to improve these individual legal systems, but such improvements must not overlook the deep value of the *macro-level* system of law in a nation (i.e., its constitution and foundational statutes, enshrining its basic rights and freedoms).

---

[106] See WILLIS, *supra* note 103, at 39-40, 50, 103-28 (analyzing Keynesian and grass-roots approaches).

[107] TAMANAHA, *supra* note 105.

[108] Not meaning *individual,* as in persons, but *separate* (and yet, this doesn't exactly capture the meaning either, as these separate legal fields are also interconnected). It's best perhaps to consider these as similar to the individual subjects one studies in law school, as indicated in the list in the text above. I refer to these as individual, internal legal systems in that sense.

I am referring to a foundational legal structure that should honor and recognize things like property, inheritance rights, marital rights, and the freedom to open a business, or get an education, in the first place. These basic rights and structural freedoms constitute the subject matter which the individual, internal fields of law above are supposed to develop. Without assurance in law (at a nation's macro-level), of these fundamental rights and structures, such individual legal fields would not even exist.[109] Some countries' legal systems do not support these fundamental structures and rights (see Communism above). A simple way to depict this vital, fundamental, macro-level legal structure in a nation, is with a square (i.e., it's a framework, which can vary in strength among nations):

WEAK   STRONG

Fig 11.3. Basic Legal Foundation/Framework (BLF)

Combining that BLF, then, with improvements in individual, internal areas of law (see examples above), we would get a picture that would look something like this (Fig. 11.4), in which each of the maze-like lines represents a discrete *micro-level* internal legal system (contracts, torts, civil procedure, inheritance, tax law, etc.), and the square (perimeter) represents the *macro-level* BLF in a nation:

---

[109] There would be no internal system of *contract law*, if people had no freedom of contract in the first place; or, there would be no point in a *tort law system*, if a duty of care to one's neighbors (and the right of the latter to be secure in his person and property, etc.) is disregarded from the start; or no *crimes of stealing* without property rights; and so on.

Basic Legal Framework (BLF)

Internal, Individual Legal Systems (contracts, torts, admin., inheritance law, etc.)

Fig 11.4. Combination of a BLF & Individual, Internal Legal Systems

The trick in constitutional democracies is to have good individual, internal legal systems, operating in these economies, in a sufficient balance. Too much legal regulation (too many inside lines, and too thick) can stifle or smother economic growth and development; too little regulation can lead to chaos (like the soccer game having lots of players but missing some key rules, or a referee).

I usually test this idea with students, asking them which of these next two diagrams depicts the best legal situation for achieving economic and social development and success, assuming people want to move in life from point A (a starting point) to B (increasing economic and social growth).

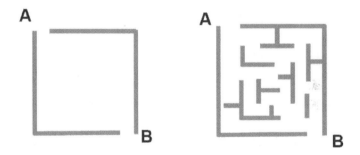

Fig 11.5 Two Different Legal Systems: which one best serves Economic and Social Growth?

If you, like many students, pick the empty square, that would be incorrect. If sensible, internal legal systems are lacking in a society (the square is empty), the result is anarchy, not growth. Instead of having the **Rule of Law** (ROL) operating in society to create order and growth, the only thing operating in a legal vacuum is **Power (Rule of Man)**, by those who have it and can use it. It is often arbitrary and cruel (consider a dictator vs. rule of law). A good society needs both a just *basic legal framework* (BLF), and sensible *individual, internal legal systems*.

A good definition of ROL is this: *the restriction of the arbitrary exercise of power by subordinating it to well-defined and established laws.*[110] I would simply add a change to this definition's end to read: . . . *established laws that are just*. Having laws that are *just* (and how we determine that), is the whole point of the earlier chapters in this Study Guide. What is the point of having ROL, if the Law part of that is not infused with the stuff of justice in the first place? To avoid rule by power, we need a *just* **Rule of Law** (ROL).[111]

However, the diagrams above, such as Fig 11.2 (law coming alongside economic development), and Fig. 11.4 (maze square, showing both a basic legal structure and individual legal systems) are two dimensional and disconnected. We should combine these to get a more dynamic model of law *coming alongside* and *serving natural economic growth*, and showing this happening through *good, individual, internal legal systems, operating within a strong legal framework* (the square foundation).

A final diagram combining these should look something like this:

---

[110] *Rule of Law*, Oxford English Dictionary (2018), https://en.oxforddictionaries.com/definition/rule_of_law.; *see also* World Justice Project, World Justice Report, https://worldjusticeproject.org/about-us/overview/what-rule-law (last visited July 31, 2018) [hereinafter WJP] (involving a four-part practical definition of ROL as: Accountability, Just Laws, an Open Government, and Valid Dispute Resolution (a judicial function), and utilizing a Rule of Law Index, based on nine factors). Note: citation here is not an endorsement of all WJP's political positions.

[111] While scholars have struggled to ascertain just how (or *if*) ROL can impact economic development, one thing is clear: *sustainable economic growth and development will not happen in a lawless society ruled by individual power.* WJP, *supra* note 110; *see also Prov.* 14:34 (*righteousness exalts a nation, but sin condemns any people*). Economic and social growth is also not going happen in a society torn by strife and civil war (consider Syria currently), and this is likely what one gets with rule under sheer power, instead of by standards of good law.

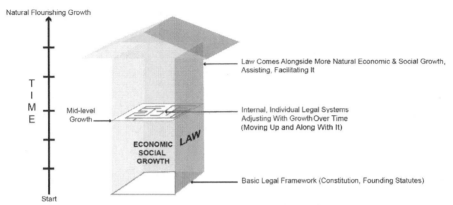

Fig 11.6 Final diagram of Law Assisting Economic and Social Growth

It should help in Fig. 11.6 to picture the square maze as a dynamic plane moving up in time with society (i.e., like an elevator or lift), toward increasing economic growth and flourishing, with individual legal systems within it adapting to changes necessary for growth over that time. The framework undergirds the society and its economy, but the individual legal systems within it move alongside, accompanying and impacting developmental changes in society at any level.[112]

Scripture and Skeptics

Some of the skeptics of L and D, including as to the estimated value of ROL for economic and social growth, I believe are ignoring a couple of key issues which undoubtedly affects their grim assessment.[113] This overlooking is either ignorant or intentional (some sensitive issues, perhaps, they seek to avoid). First, in giving law a low score in facilitating development (again, citing many underdeveloped countries with lots of laws), they seem to ignore that the success of law, and ROL, depends on its ***enforcement***. Law is only as useful as its implementation – an essential part of law itself (see Ecclesiastes. 8:11). The issuing of many laws, even good ones, holds no terror for unjust rulers.

---

[112] *See* TAMANAHA, *supra* note 105, at 214, 219 (system adaptations). The systems could also descend lower through war and civil strife.

[113] *Id.* at 212-18.

It's the enforcement of them, the actual *Rule of Law*, that does. Commentators confound the lack of enforcement of law as a defect in law and development itself. That is not the problem, sin and corruption are, and that leads to the second point.

Second, many scholars are secularists, and won't discuss corruption and sin very directly (corruption gets air time, but not sin so much, when really they are the same thing; also, corruption in governing is a specific subset of sin). In a legal-political sense, corruption is simply the antithesis of ROL (assuming good law is already present). Many countries are very aware of their corruption issues (Indonesia, Cambodia, and various places I have visited). What the leadership in many counties is often not so aware of, is the stark causal relationship existing between corruption and poverty. **Corruption causes poverty, and it keeps developing countries poor.**[114] The worn-out, inverse adage "poverty causes corruption," is simply insufficient to capture the issue. See the diagram available through a link in Appendix VII (Link 11.1), showing how corruption causes and worsens poverty in a vicious circle at national (macro) and local/community (micro) levels, simultaneously.

Since sin is the source of corruption, the problem of corruption can't really be addressed without also addressing sin, specifically the sinful, selfish aspects of fallen human nature, which government leadership is not immune from. Legal scholars, especially secular ones, do not like to talk about this, although it is the core issue. It is the source of corruption, which so badly harms economic growth.

Gospel and Development

In the final analysis, good and just societies are the result of good and just people living in them. And people become good and just when they are transformed internally by Jesus Christ, through the preaching and acceptance of his gospel of salvation. That's why no social transformation in society is likely to be genuine, deep, and sustainable without the preaching of and obedience to the gospel of Jesus Christ, and His power at work. It can't simply be left up to good laws (and besides, how would they be accepted by a wicked populace anyway?). This is the

---

[114] *See Proverbs* 14:34. See also World Bank studies, including those cited below.

key ingredient many secularist L and D scholars are too shy (or too hostile) to admit and discuss.[115]

Impediments to ROL and Economic Growth – An Evil Trio

This section identifies three of the more serious impediments known, that strongly inhibit ROL, and so retard economic and social growth. It should be clear how each shows an infestation of the sin and corruption issues discussed immediately above (since each is antithetical to the *rule of just law*). I will end with some sources for you to read supporting each issue.

(1) **Violence.** It is especially a problem in poorer communities, where public justice systems and law enforcement are weak or non-existent. In *The Locust Effect*, authors Victor Boutros and Gary Haugen make a strong case for how violence in local communities, having corrupt or inept police and justice systems, keep those communities bullied and economically deprived (except for the bullies).[116] This diagram from International Justice Mission (IJM) typifies the problems of corruption and broken public justice systems (PJS) in developing countries, which Christian students and advocates are called to repair, so that justice in communities can again, *flow like a river.* (Amos 5:24)

A Broken Public Justice System Pipeline

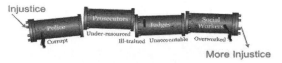

Fig. 11.7 Broken Criminal Justice Systems © 2015 International Justice Mission

---

[115] Intercessory prayer for justice is another spiritual solution to the problems of sin and poverty, and is part of a growing movement among advocates in the world, supported by this author.

[116] GARY A. HAUGEN AND VICTOR BOUTROS, THE LOCUST EFFECT, WHY THE END OF POVERTY REQUIRES THE END OF VIOLENCE (2014) (*see id.* at 101, citing World Bank studies).

Consider also the impact of violence on a national scale; i.e., how corruption in government leadership can easily provoke civil unrest, riots, and war. In such a violent environment, economic and social growth is nearly impossible. In short, violence signals a lack of ROL.

(2) **Corruption in the form of Bribery and Extortion.** Although perhaps seeming less dramatic than actual violence, this sort of corruption is very widespread, and even a cultural norm in some places in the developing world. It is so common, it may wreak the most systemic havoc in the long term, and in terms of economic numbers, in the developing world.[117] Scripture notes this problem, speaking candidly of its distortion of justice and the impact this has. Scriptures on extortion and bribery, and their distorting effects, are listed in Appendix VI.

(3) **Overwhelming Administrative Bureaucracy, "Red Tape."** This is a subtle kind of corruption in the form of inefficiency, including an attitude of lack of cooperation and laziness, mostly exhibited by government employees and officials in many nations. This may not end in lost lives or stolen goods as in the case of violence, but it can surely thwart new small businesses from starting and crush a positive entrepreneurial spirit, often out of sheer frustration in being able to get anything accomplished. It is very widespread in the developing world. Economist Hernando de Soto captured this problem in sections of his book, *The Mystery of Capital* (see at 18-28). A slide-diagram, available as a link in Appendix VII (Link 11.2), depicts the problem (see the left side of that diagram on Administrative Legal Systems (ALS)).

---

[117] KIRK HAMILTON ET AL., WHERE IS THE WEALTH OF NATIONS?, THE WORLD BANK (2006), *available at* http://siteresources.worldbank.org/INTEEI/214578-1110886258964/20748034/All.pdf (justice systems are of greater importance than educational systems to increase national wealth) (*cited in* HAUGEN AND BOUTROS, *supra* note 116, at 155).

In short, impediments (1) and (2) above portray *lawlessness*, or an absence of a good and just law (i.e., ROL); while (3) is about *too much* so-called *law* (i.e., the suffocating effects of over-regulation, or the inexplicably annoying, hyper-technical application of red tape).[118]

Suggested Sources

I have mentioned some of these above as well.

(1) Gary A. Haugen and Victor Boutros, *The Locust Effect, Why the End of Poverty Requires the End of Violence* (2014), on how lawless violence and broken public justice systems in developing communities inhibit their economic growth, and perpetuate poverty.

(2) Wayne Grudem and Barry Asmus, *The Poverty of Nations, A Sustainable Solution* (2013), on how several factors, including sin and corruption, and ineffective forms of government impact the poverty of countries (70+ factors considered).[119]

(3) Hernando de Soto, *The Mystery of Capital, Why Capitalism Triumphs in the West and Fails Everywhere Else* (2000), on how red tape and legal systems lacking in sense impact property rights of the poor and impede growth (*see id.* at 18-28).

---

[118] Indonesia (this author's present home), is full of real-life stories of both problems. In the same city of Jakarta we see numerous cases of a government ministry being hyper-technical in not approving business licenses (nitpicking, and harassing with enforcement of spurious rules). This is often because the owner refused to pay an extorted fee or bribe (also common in traffic stops), and countless white collar criminals or other violators going unpunished because they do bribe (ignoring the law).

[119] Although written by Christian scholars, a colleague believes this work should give greater attention to sin and relational poverty (such as lack of fathers in the home, broken families, etc.). Such issues are certainly serious, root-level impediments to flourishing.

DISCUSSION QUESTIONS:

1. What were the earlier misconceptions of law and development? What is the current thinking of how law and development should work?

2. From the two squares noted in Fig. 11.5, one blank and one mazed, why is the blank one more difficult in achieving economic growth and order?

3. What are three impediments to the Rule of Law mentioned above? Do you see these impediments at work in your community and country?

4. How can we improve our justice and legal systems to be less corrupt? Specifically, what legal efforts could help? Consider the following initiatives:

    a) Improving legislative and enforcement efforts to stop anti-competitive (anti-trust) commercial behavior, including prosecution of white-collar criminals, and attempts to crack down on cartels and oligopolies.

    b) Improving "internal affairs" (anti-corruption units) for government ministries and bureaucracies in your country (holding them accountable).

c) Passing "whistle-blower" laws for those who expose corruption against businesses, government, sometimes religious, and other institutions (if you don't know what these laws are, look them up in U.S. and other systems).

d) Conducting ethics, competency, and other training programs for judges, police, and government employees in general (in the latter case, consider how that might stop shameful sex-trafficking and other violations against vulnerable people); i.e., "soft law" efforts (can these improve things?).

5. How can we strive to maintain our Christian behaviour in a corrupt system? How do we impart the right values to our clients also? (See Proverbs 22:1)

PRAYER POINTS:

1. Pray that you would keep your heart pure and accept no bribe.
2. Pray that God would give you grace to not engage in extortion if you are in a position of power over someone.
3. Pray for the justice system in your country that there would be honest judges, qualified prosecutors, and equipped advocates.
4. Pray for the initiatives above (in question 4) to counter corruption, and improve rule of <u>just</u> law in your community and country.

PART III

A CAREER CALLING IN LAW AND JUSTICE

Chapter 12

ADVOCATES INTERNATIONAL: DOING JUSTICE WITH COMPASSION

This is what the Lord Almighty said: "Administer true justice; show
mercy and compassion to one another."
(Zechariah 7:9)

I HOPE THROUGH the above you have seen the importance and value of law and justice in society. You may even be considering a career in law or government, or otherwise simply in doing justice. Some information in this chapter is admittedly aimed at attorneys, but all of it should assist anyone interested in justice.

The legal profession is ultimately about advancing justice on the earth, which is a way to love our neighbor (our fellow man) (Luke 10:27). If you are thinking about becoming a lawyer, but honestly think your joining might increase the level of *injustice* on the earth, please don't join (you should instead repent). As a Christian, you should see your work as kingdom work, for Christ, advancing its influence in the earth, as if God were working through you, and you are the *mask* He is wearing to impart some of His love and common grace on humankind.[120]

---

[120] MICHAEL P. SCHUTT, REDEEMING LAW, CHRISTIAN CALLING AND THE LEGAL PROFESSION 46-54 (2007) (discussing Luther's view that God wears us, and our careers, as His masks, supplying common grace to humankind – a non-salvific grace); *see also* Matt. 5:45 (God shines His sun, and sends the rain, on the just and the unjust).

Career Resources

I want to commend two books on this final topic of your calling in law and justice work.

1. Joseph G. Allegretti, *The Lawyer's Calling, Christian Faith and Legal Practice* (1996) (only 140 pages).
2. Michael P. Schutt, *Redeeming Law, Christian Calling and the Legal Profession* (2007).

It is important to know these sources, because many Christian students are unsure whether they can or should practice law. I will defer to the above works, primarily, but will here offer some insights from Allegretti's book on this important issue.

Christ and *the Code*

In short, Allegretti identifies four positions Christians have taken in response to modern-day lawyering, which he calls, *the Code*. This Code refers to the worldly system of lawyering, which is to win at all costs: lawyers are hired to achieve the objectives of their clients at all costs, even if it means working toward injustice, in order to get their desired result. While most bar associations do not approve of this style of ethics, the Code teaches us to do what we have to in order to win, even if our actions are a little crooked, malicious or unkind (if not illegal), and if we can get away with it. It's the worldly way.

Allegretti observes four responses by Christians to this way of thinking, as captured in this diagram (the term *standard vision* below, is the same as *the Code* in Allegretti's work):

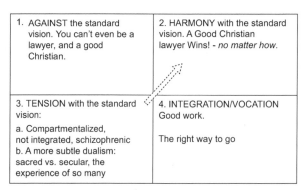

Fig. 12.1 Four responses to the 'win at all costs' standard vision (a/k/a, 'the Code')

(1) Christ Against The Code (a/k/a the 'Standard Vision'). In this view Christians don't think they can practice law because it requires dishonest or hostile tactics (despite ethics codes against this), including lying, bribing and nasty pressure tactics. They feel it's a bad business, and so leave the profession.

(2) Christ In Harmony With The Code. In this view, Christians don't mind sometimes resorting to dirty, or unethical tactics, since it can help them win, gaining them a strong reputation, and this is supposed to make them shine for Jesus. Christians should have the testimony of "winners," the argument goes, so the ethical breaches are considered worth it. This is just an excuse, however, to justify a lack of integrity. Instead of bringing glory to God, by winning, it does the opposite. Combat and winning in law must still be done in a way that honors Christ.

(3) Christ In Tension With The Code. In this situation, Christian practitioners may know they are being dishonest, ungodly, or unethical in some ways in their practice, but say that's just the way it is. "It's part of the culture," they say. So, they try to make up for it with other Christian service in their life (at church, etc.).

This thinking is unsustainable in its tension. Eventually, a person will either repent (see (4) next), or they will slip back into (2), trying to justify their unethical conduct as good for winning (shown by the arrow reverting back to (2)).

I have added a similar kind of behavior here (see 3.b. in diagram above), that I think is representative of many practitioners (it was for this author). It may not be an intentional double life, but it is still holds a harmful kind of dualism: It is the false dichotomy practitioners think they have, of separating life into a *secular* job, and *sacred, spiritual* work, such as at church. This view fails to grasp how lawyering and similar work should be handled in Christ's kingdom, serving people *through it*. They falsely think spiritual work is done by pastors and missionaries ("fulltime" ministers), when in fact their work is also spiritual, if it does good and serves others (loving one's neighbor, Luke 10:27), but which they often fail to see. That view cheapens the sacredness of work, as God's calling, even on a regular job (I am obviously not talking about a job that is inherently illicit, like selling drugs, or sex). *All good work of the Christian called to it is God's work.*

107

(4) Christ Transforming The Code. In this view, we as Christian lawyers, legal professionals, and students seek to transform or improve the legal system and improve justice. This is the right way, and glorifies God, even if those embracing it face persecution or insults. It is part of *redeeming* the legal system in your community.[121]

Commercial Law or Human Rights Law
(Pre-Victim vs Post-Victim Justice)

As a student, you may not become a human rights, or public interest lawyer, and do justice in that way (see Proverbs 31:8-9). That's perfectly alright. If you are engaged in providing good legal services, advancing healthy economic enterprises in the corporate or business law fields, you are actually improving your nation's economic health. This is good as it reduces conditions that lead to sex-trafficking, slavery, and other exploitation of vulnerable (usually poorer) people.

I shall call this **pre-victim justice**, because it helps prevent or reduce victims of human rights abuses. Yes, good commercial law can help do this. If you are called to that kind of commercial legal work, it has an impact on justice. It is a way, through the law, to prevent victims; it helps prevent people from suffering the harms and consequences of injustice.

The work of those who help the victims of injustice and its consequences directly, I shall call **post-victim justice**. This is certainly necessary in our sinful world, but much of the suffering that creates victims is preventable by the exercise of initial justice in other, regular areas of law (in commerce, trade, education, labor, family, agriculture, natural resources, investment, and in similar areas of law, which can build nations).

It is still a good idea to get involved in other, post-victim justice advocacy, such as helping the poor and needy, and combatting sex-trafficking and other social ills to help victims of injustice, even if as a volunteer. In your career, you may also have pro-bono service opportunities, or required hours to fulfill, and many good and godly opportunities exist. Corporate Social Responsibility (CSR) is a similar example of this.

---

[121] A complete slide show on this material is available to the reader through a link in Appendix VII (12.1). See also the books above for more information.

Advocates International's Work

This Study Guide was written in part to help students, attorneys, churches and simply interested persons, connected in some way with a local Christian legal society or support group, and with Advocates International (AI). Its goal is to help advocates understand and improve justice in their communities, in a biblical approach. AI seeks to bear witness to Jesus Christ through the legal profession.[122]

Local, National, and Regional Activities. AI has regional organizations in each of the six continents. It also has national organizations, as well as local chapters. AI's strategy is to *network regionally, organize nationally, and disciple globally.* If you can't find a local chapter in your area, maybe we can help you start one.

AI encourages all of its local chapters and groups to come together to chiefly do three things: (1) study to develop a Christian worldview on law, justice and government from books and other resources (like this one), and including online resources we make available; (2) work on one of seven advocacy projects (called Global Resource Teams, or GRTs), and AI can help connect you to some resources to help you get started on one of these (see below); and (3) enable professional mentoring and development, including skills training.

7 GRT Advocacy Project Areas. AI encourages local chapters (students, attorneys and similar professionals) to get involved in one of the following advocacy areas. We often team up with other partners for skills training and assistance to see that through. Thus, we advocate by:

(1) *Promoting the Rule of Law and Combatting Corruption.* Lack of transparency and corruption is a major systemic contributor to poverty in any nation, as discussed above. It's what keeps poor countries poor, impeding economic growth, and leading to human rights abuses (and the need for more human rights lawyers).

(2) *Protecting Religious Liberty and Freedom of Conscience.* Opponents of this include hostile secularists in the West to non-Christian antagonists, and religious extremists in the East.

---

[122] ADVOCATES INTERNATIONAL, www.advocatesinternational.org (last visited April 18, 2019).

(3) *Safeguarding Human Rights, Doing Justice for the Poor and Needy.* The poor usually lack access to justice and a good legal system. Many are exploited. Efforts to improve justice include combatting sex-trafficking, property and personal rights violations, modern day slavery, or helping refugees.

(4) *Defending the Sanctity of Life.* This includes working against abortion, infanticide, assisted suicide, euthanasia and killing of the elderly. It can also involve issues of stem cell research protections. Issues may vary with locations.

(5) *Defending Marriage and Family.* These are under attack in many cultures today, due to the violent advocacy of many LGBT activist groups, who twist the natural law to achieve a distortion of these God-given institutions (given to all). It also involves counseling to strengthen marriages and families in the church.

(6) *Peacemaking and Reconciliation.* Where possible, this can be a powerful path to healing, instead of litigation, and in some cases to avoid war. AI seeks to engage in peacemaking both at national/international levels involving ethnic strife, as well as in disputes among individuals, families and companies.

(7) *Praying (Intercession) for Justice.* AI is part of an international prayer movement. It also encourages local, national and regional prayer networks to combat the above issues, and improve justice on the earth.

AI's Partners

To achieve many of the above goals and activities, AI co-labors in partnerships with some key, stellar organizations. Cooperation includes training with these groups, and enables participants (students, attorneys, judges, academics, or anyone seeking to advocate for justice), to get involved with skilled individuals already doing work in these areas, to make their own work even more effective. Such partnerships assist with AI's professional development of its affiliates. Some of AI's partners include:

(1) **International Justice Mission (IJM).** IJM is dedicated to justice efforts like anti-trafficking and combatting human slavery, and other systemic human rights abuses.

(2) ADF (Alliance Defending Freedom) International. ADF International is skilled in areas of religious liberty, sanctity of life, and marriage and family, especially. ADF has a training partnership with AI constituents.

(3) Faith and Law Around the Globe (FLAG). FLAG equips attorneys and students for sharing the good news, spiritual growth, integrity, and influencing the legal community.

Other International Organizations (IOs) and NGOs, some Christian and some not, also work with us, such as the International Organization of Migration (IOM) in Indonesia, Open Doors (Christian), and others. You can check out some of these and more on AI's website, and also find Christian resources to help you learn more about Christianity, law and justice, like this Study Guide.

DISCUSSION QUESTIONS:

1. As Christians and up and coming lawyers or legal professionals, how can we uphold our ethics in a Christ-like manner? When there is tension between these two identities, how can we transform the Code Allegretti describes?

2. What is the distinction between *pre-victim* and *post-victim justice*? Is there a sense in which each is a viable calling to justice and serving Jesus Christ, and can the former help reduce the need for the latter?

3. What are some organizational partners Advocates International has?

4. Which of the seven above areas of service are you most interested in?

5. How will you take a next step to get involved (start or join a local chapter or student group, consider a project in your area, etc.)?

PRAYER POINTS:

1. Remembering that you are made in the image of God, pray that your calling would be clear.
2. Pray for advocates around the world, especially in countries where they don't have freedom to worship.
3. Pray for the justice system in your community and country to be transformed.

Happy Advocating for Jesus, in His Kingdom!

APPENDICES

APPENDIX I

Scripture Verses on Justice
and Acting Justly

Scripture Verses on Justice (emphasis is this author's)

1. Genesis 49:16. *Dan will provide **justice** for his people as one of the tribes of Israel.*
2. Exodus 23:2. *Do not follow the crowd in doing wrong. When you give testimony in a lawsuit, do not pervert **justice** by siding with the crowd . . . .*
3. Exodus 23:6. *Do not deny **justice** to your poor people in their lawsuits.*
4. Leviticus 19:15. *Do not pervert **justice**; do not show partiality to the poor or favoritism to the great, but judge your neighbor fairly.*
5. Deuteronomy 16:19. *Do not pervert **justice** or show partiality. Do not accept a bribe, for a bribe blinds the eyes of the wise and twists the words of the innocent.*
6. Deuteronomy 16:20. *Follow **justice** and justice alone, so that you may live and possess the land the LORD your God is giving you.*
7. Deuteronomy 24:17. *Do not deprive the foreigner or the fatherless of **justice**, or take the cloak of the widow as a pledge.*
8. Deuteronomy 27:19. *"Cursed is anyone who withholds **justice** from the foreigner, the fatherless or the widow." Then all the people shall say, "Amen!"*
9. 1 Samuel 8:3. *But his sons did not follow his ways. They turned aside after dishonest gain and accepted bribes and perverted **justice**.*
10. 2 Samuel 15:4. *And Absalom would add, "If only I were appointed judge in the land! Then everyone who has a complaint or case could come to me and I would see that they receive **justice**."*
11. 2 Samuel 15:6. *Absalom behaved in this way toward all the Israelites who came to the king asking for **justice**, and so he stole the hearts of the people of Israel.*
12. 1 Kings 3:11. *So God said to him, "Since you have asked for this and not for long life or wealth for yourself, nor have asked for the death of your enemies but for discernment in administering **justice** . . . ."*
13. 1 Kings 3:28. *When all Israel heard the verdict the king had given, they held the king in awe, because they saw that he had wisdom from God to administer **justice**.*

14. 1 Kings 7:7. *He built the throne hall, the Hall of **Justice**, where he was to judge, and he covered it with cedar from floor to ceiling.*

15. 1 Kings 10:9. *Praise be to the LORD your God, who has delighted in you and placed you on the throne of Israel. Because of the LORD's eternal love for Israel, he has made you king to maintain **justice** and righteousness.* (See also 2 Chronicles 9:8 (same).)

16. Ezra 7:25. *And you, Ezra, in accordance with the wisdom of your God, which you possess, appoint magistrates and judges to administer **justice** to all the people of Trans-Euphrates— all who know the laws of your God. And you are to teach any who do not know them.*

17. Esther 1:13. *Since it was customary for the king to consult experts in matters of law and **justice**, he spoke with the wise men who understood the times.*

18. Job 8:3. *Does God pervert **justice**? Does the Almighty pervert what is right?*

19. Job 9:19. *If it is a matter of strength, he is mighty! And if it is a matter of **justice**, who can challenge him?*

20. Job 19:7. *Though I cry, "Violence!" I get no response; though I call for help, there is no **justice**.*

21. Job 27:2. *As surely as God lives, who has denied me **justice**, the Almighty, who has made my life bitter . . . .*

22. Job 29:14. *I put on righteousness as my clothing; **justice** was my robe and my turban.*

23. Job 31:13-14. *If I have denied **justice** to any of my servants, whether male or female, when they had a grievance against me . . . what will I do . . . ?*

24. Job 34:5. *Job says, "I am innocent, but God denies me **justice** . . . ."*

25. Job 34:12. *It is unthinkable that God would do wrong, that the Almighty would pervert **justice**.*

26. Job 34:17. *Can someone who hates **justice** govern? Will you condemn the just and mighty One?*

27. Job 36:3. *I get my knowledge from afar; I will ascribe **justice** to my Maker.*

28. Job 36:17. *But now you are laden with the judgment due the wicked; judgment and **justice** have taken hold of you.*

29. Job 37:23. *The Almighty is beyond our reach and exalted in power; in his **justice** and great righteousness, he does not oppress.*

30. Job 40:8. *Would you discredit my **justice**? Would you condemn me to justify yourself?*

31. Psalm 7:6. *Arise, LORD, in your anger; rise up against the rage of my enemies. Awake, my God; decree **justice**.*

32. Psalm 9:8. *He rules the world in **righteousness** and **judges** the peoples with equity.*
33. Psalm 9:16. *The LORD is known by his acts of **justice**; the wicked are ensnared by the work of their hands.*
34. Psalm 11:7. *For the LORD is righteous, he loves **justice**; the upright will see his face.*
35. Psalm 33:5. *The LORD loves righteousness and **justice**; the earth is full of his unfailing love.*
36. Psalm 36:6. *Your righteousness is like the highest mountains, your **justice** like the great deep. You, LORD, preserve both people and animals.*
37. Psalm 45:4. *In your majesty ride forth victoriously in the cause of truth, humility and **justice**; let your right hand achieve awesome deeds.*
38. Psalm 45:6. *Your throne, O God, will last for ever and ever; a scepter of **justice** will be the scepter of your kingdom.*
39. Psalm 50:6. *And the heavens proclaim his righteousness, for he is a God of **justice**.*
40. Psalm 72:1. *Of Solomon. Endow the king with your **justice**, O God, the royal son with your righteousness.*
41. Psalm 72:2. *May he judge your people in righteousness, your afflicted ones with **justice**.*
42. Psalm 89:14. *Righteousness and **justice** are the foundation of your throne; love and faithfulness go before you.*
43. Psalm 97:2. *Clouds and thick darkness surround him; righteousness and **justice** are the foundation of his throne.*
44. Psalm 99:4. *The King is mighty, he loves **justice**— you have established equity; in Jacob you have done what is **just** and right.*
45. Psalm 101:1. *Of David. A psalm. I will sing of your love and **justice**; to you, LORD, I will sing praise.*
46. Psalm 103:6. *The LORD works righteousness and **justice** for all the oppressed.*
47. Psalm 112:5. *Good will come to those who are generous and lend freely, who conduct their affairs with **justice**.*
48. Psalm 140:12. *I know that the LORD secures **justice** for the poor and upholds the cause of the needy.*
49. Proverbs 8:20. *I walk in the way of righteousness, along the paths of **justice**,*
50. Proverbs 16:10. *The lips of a king speak as an oracle, and his mouth does not betray **justice**.*
51. Proverbs 17:23. *The wicked accept bribes in secret to pervert the course of **justice**.*

52. Proverbs 18:5. *It is not good to be partial to the wicked and so deprive the innocent of justice.*

53. Proverbs 19:28. *A corrupt witness mocks at justice, and the mouth of the wicked gulps down evil.*

54. Proverbs 21:15. *When justice is done, it brings joy to the righteous but terror to evildoers.*

55. Proverbs 29:4. *By justice a king gives a country stability, but those who are greedy for bribes tear it down.*

56. Proverbs 29:7. *The righteous care about justice for the poor, but the wicked have no such concern.*

57. Proverbs 29:26. *Many seek an audience with a ruler, but it is from the LORD that one gets justice.*

58. Ecclesiastes 3:16. *And I saw something else under the sun: In the place of judgment— wickedness was there, in the place of justice—wickedness was there.*

59. Ecclesiastes 5:8. *If you see the poor oppressed in a district, and justice and rights denied, do not be surprised at such things; for one official is eyed by a higher one, and over them both are others higher still.*

60. Isaiah 1:17. *Learn to do right; seek justice. Defend the oppressed. Take up the cause of the fatherless; plead the case of the widow.*

61. Isaiah 1:21. *See how the faithful city has become a prostitute! She once was full of justice; righteousness used to dwell in her— but now murderers!*

62. Isaiah 1:27. *Zion will be delivered with justice, her penitent ones with righteousness.*

63. Isaiah 5:7. *The vineyard of the LORD Almighty is the nation of Israel, and the people of Judah are the vines he delighted in. And he looked for justice, but saw bloodshed; for righteousness, but heard cries of distress.*

64. Isaiah 5:16. *But the LORD Almighty will be exalted by his justice, and the holy God will be proved holy by his righteous acts.*

65. Isaiah 5:23. *who acquit the guilty for a bribe, but deny justice to the innocent.*

66. Isaiah 9:7. *Of the greatness of his government and peace there will be no end. He will reign on David's throne and over his kingdom, establishing and upholding it with justice and righteousness from that time on and forever. The zeal of the LORD Almighty will accomplish this.*

67. Isaiah 10:2. *to deprive the poor of their rights and withhold justice from the oppressed of my people, making widows their prey and robbing the fatherless.*

68. Isaiah 11:4. *but with righteousness he will judge the needy, with* **justice** *he will give decisions for the poor of the earth. He will strike the earth with the rod of his mouth; with the breath of his lips he will slay the wicked.*

69. Isaiah 16:5. *In love a throne will be established; in faithfulness a man will sit on it— one from the house of David— one who in judging seeks* **justice** *and speeds the cause of righteousness.*

70. Isaiah 28:6. *He will be a spirit of* **justice** *to the one who sits in judgment, a source of strength to those who turn back the battle at the gate.*

71. Isaiah 28:17. *I will make* **justice** *the measuring line and righteousness the plumb line; hail will sweep away your refuge, the lie, and water will overflow your hiding place.*

72. Isaiah 29:21. *those who with a word make someone out to be guilty, who ensnare the defender in court and with false testimony deprive the innocent of* **justice.**

73. Isaiah 30:18. *Yet the LORD longs to be gracious to you; therefore he will rise up to show you compassion. For the LORD is a God of* **justice.** *Blessed are all who wait for him!*

74. Isaiah 32:1. *[The Kingdom of Righteousness] See, a king will reign in righteousness and rulers will rule with* **justice.**

75. Isaiah 32:16. *The LORD's* **justice** *will dwell in the desert, his righteousness live in the fertile field.*

76. Isaiah 33:5. *The LORD is exalted, for he dwells on high; he will fill Zion with his* **justice** *and righteousness.*

77. Isaiah 42:1. *Here is my servant, whom I uphold, my chosen one in whom I delight; I will put my Spirit on him, and he will bring* **justice** *to the nations.*

78. Isaiah 42:3-4. *³A bruised reed he will not break, and a smoldering wick he will not snuff out. In faithfulness he will bring forth* **justice;** *⁴he will not falter or be discouraged till he establishes* **justice** *on earth. In his teaching the islands will put their hope.*

79. Isaiah 51:4. *Listen to me, my people; hear me, my nation: Instruction will go out from me; my* **justice** *will become a light to the nations.*

80. Isaiah 51:5. *My righteousness draws near speedily, my salvation is on the way, and my arm will bring* **justice** *to the nations. The islands will look to me and wait in hope for my arm.*

81. Isaiah 56:1. *This is what the LORD says: "Maintain* **justice** *and do what is right, for my salvation is close at hand and my righteousness will soon be revealed."*

82. Isaiah 59:4. *No one calls for **justice**; no one pleads a case with integrity. They rely on empty arguments, they utter lies; they conceive trouble and give birth to evil.*

83. Isaiah 59:8. *The way of peace they do not know; there is no **justice** in their paths. They have turned them into crooked roads; no one who walks along them will know peace.*

84. Isaiah 59:9. *So **justice** is far from us, and righteousness does not reach us. We look for light, but all is darkness; for brightness, but we walk in deep shadows.*

85. Isaiah 59:11. *We all growl like bears; we moan mournfully like doves. We look for **justice**, but find none; for deliverance, but it is far away.*

86. Isaiah 59:14. *So **justice** is driven back, and righteousness stands at a distance; truth has stumbled in the streets, honesty cannot enter.*

87. Isaiah 59:15. *Truth is nowhere to be found, and whoever shuns evil becomes a prey. The LORD looked and was displeased that there was no **justice**.*

88. Isaiah 61:8. *For I, the LORD, love **justice**; I hate robbery and wrongdoing. In my faithfulness I will reward my people and make an everlasting covenant with them.*

89. Jeremiah 5:28. *Their evil deeds have no limit; they do not seek **justice**. They do not promote the case of the fatherless; they do not defend the just cause of the poor.*

90. Jeremiah 9:24. *I am the LORD, who exercises kindness, **justice** and righteousness on earth, for in these I delight . . . .*

91. Jeremiah 12:1. *You are always righteous, LORD, when I bring a case before you. Yet I would speak with you about your **justice**: Why does the way of the wicked prosper? Why do all the faithless live at ease?*

92. Jeremiah 21:12. *This is what the LORD says to you, house of David: "Administer **justice** every morning; rescue from the hand of the oppressor the one who has been robbed, or my wrath will break out and burn like fire because of the evil you have done— burn with no one to quench it."*

93. Lamentations 3:35-36. *[35][T]o deprive people their rights before the Most High, [36]to deprive them of **justice**— would not the Lord see such things?*

94. Ezekiel 22:29. *The people of the land practice extortion and commit robbery; they oppress the poor and needy and mistreat the foreigner, denying them **justice**.*

95. Ezekiel 34:16. *I will search for the lost and bring back the strays. I will bind up the injured and strengthen the weak, but the sleek and the strong I will destroy. I will shepherd the flock with **justice**.*

96. Hosea 2:19. *I will betroth you to me forever; I will betroth you in righteousness and **justice**, in love and compassion.*

97. Hosea 12:6. *But you must return to your God; maintain love and **justice**, and wait for your God always.*

98. Amos 2:7. *They trample on the heads of the poor as on the dust of the ground and deny **justice** to the oppressed. Father and son use the same girl and so profane my holy name.*

99. Amos 5:7. *There are those who turn **justice** into bitterness and cast righteousness to the ground.*

100. Amos 5:10. *There are those who hate the one who upholds **justice** in court and detest the one who tells the truth.*

101. Amos 5:12. *For I know how many are your offenses and how great your sins. There are those who oppress the innocent and take bribes and deprive the poor of **justice** in the courts.*

102. Amos 5:15. *Hate evil, love good; maintain **justice** in the courts. Perhaps the LORD God Almighty will have mercy on the remnant of Joseph.*

103. Amos 5:24. *But let **justice** roll on like a river, righteousness like a never-failing stream!*

104. Amos 6:12. *Do horses run on the rocky crags? Does one plow the sea with oxen? But you have turned **justice** into poison and the fruit of righteousness into bitterness—*

105. Micah 3:1. *Then I said, "Listen, you leaders of Jacob, you rulers of Israel. Should you not embrace **justice** . . . ?"*

106. Micah 3:8-9.[8] *But as for me, I am filled with power, with the Spirit of the LORD, and with **justice** and might, to declare to Jacob his transgression, to Israel his sin.* [9]*Hear this, you leaders of Jacob, you rulers of Israel, who despise **justice** and distort all that is right . . . .*

107. Habakkuk 1:4. *Therefore the law is paralyzed, and **justice** never prevails. The wicked hem in the righteous, so that **justice** is perverted.*

108. Zephaniah 3:5. *The LORD within her is righteous; he does no wrong. Morning by morning he dispenses his **justice**, and every new day he does not fail, yet the unrighteous know no shame.*

109. Zechariah 7:9. *This is what the LORD Almighty said: "Administer true **justice**; show mercy and compassion to one another."*

110. Malachi 2:17. *You have wearied the LORD with your words. "How have we wearied him?" you ask. By saying, "All who do evil are good in the eyes of the LORD, and he is pleased with them" or "Where is the God of **justice**?"*

111. Malachi 3:5. *"So I will come to put you on trial. I will be quick to testify against sorcerers, adulterers and perjurers, against those who defraud laborers of their wages, who oppress the widows and the fatherless, and deprive the foreigners among you of **justice**, but do not fear me," says the LORD Almighty.*

112. Matthew 12:18. *Here is my servant whom I have chosen, the one I love, in whom I delight; I will put my Spirit on him, and he will proclaim **justice** to the nations.*

113. Matthew 12:20. *A bruised reed he will not break, and a smoldering wick he will not snuff out, till he has brought **justice** through to victory.*

114. Matthew 23:23. *Woe to you, teachers of the law and Pharisees, you hypocrites! You give a tenth of your spices—mint, dill and cumin. But you have neglected the more important matters of the law—**justice**, mercy and faithfulness. You should have practiced the latter, without neglecting the former.*

115. Luke 11:42. *Woe to you Pharisees, because you give God a tenth of your mint, rue and all other kinds of garden herbs, but you neglect **justice** and the love of God. You should have practiced the latter without leaving the former undone.*

116. Luke 18:3-5. *And there was a widow in that town who kept coming to him with the plea, "Grant me **justice** against my adversary."* [4]*For some time he refused. . . .* "[5]*yet because this widow keeps bothering me, I will see that she gets **justice**, so that she won't eventually come and attack me!"*

117. Luke 18:7. *And will not God bring about **justice** for his chosen ones, who cry out to him day and night? Will he keep putting them off?*

118. Luke 18:8. *I tell you, he will see that they get **justice**, and quickly. However, when the Son of Man comes, will he find faith on the earth?"*

119. Acts 8:33. *In his humiliation he was deprived of **justice**. Who can speak of his descendants? For his life was taken from the earth.*

120. Acts 17:31. *For he has set a day when he will judge the world with **justice** by the man he has appointed. He has given proof of this to everyone by raising him from the dead.*

121. Acts 28:4. *When the islanders saw the snake hanging from his hand, they said to each other, "This man must be a murderer; for though he escaped from the sea, the goddess **Justice** has not allowed him to live."*

122. 2 Corinthians 7:11. *See what this godly sorrow has produced in you: what earnestness, what eagerness to clear yourselves, what indignation, what alarm, what longing, what*

concern, what readiness to see **justice** *done. At every point you have proved yourselves to be innocent in this matter.*

123. Hebrews 1:8. *But about the Son he says, "Your throne, O God, will last for ever and ever; a scepter of* **justice** *will be the scepter of your kingdom.*

124. Hebrews 11:33. *who through faith conquered kingdoms, administered* **justice**, *and gained what was promised; who shut the mouths of lions . . . .*

125. Revelation 19:11. *I saw heaven standing open and there before me was a white horse, whose rider is called Faithful and True. With* **justice** *he judges and wages war.*

Scripture Verses on Acting Justly

1. Psalm 58:1. *Do you rulers indeed speak* **justly**? *Do you judge people with equity?*

2. Psalm 106:3. *Blessed are those who act* **justly**, *who always do what is right.*

3. Jeremiah 7:5. *If you really change your ways and your actions and deal with each other* **justly**,

4. Micah 6:8. *He has shown you, O mortal, what is good. And what does the* LORD *require of you? To act* **justly** *and to love mercy and to walk humbly with your God.*

5. Luke 23:41. *We are punished* **justly**, *for we are getting what our deeds deserve. But this man has done nothing wrong.*

6. 1 Peter 2:23. *When they hurled their insults at him, he did not retaliate; when he suffered, he made no threats. Instead, he entrusted himself to him who judges* **justly**.

APPENDIX II

Supplemental Short Table on Kinds of Justice

This table is intended to help you know some of the main ideas and vocabulary associated classically with studies of justice, and for your further study. In this author's view, the vocabulary and ideas below are not necessarily absolute, nor always biblical on justice. But familiarity with this information may still be instructive and helpful in your life (see Student Handbook for more information.)

Common Categories of Justice in Humanity (Aristotle, Grotius, etc.)

TYPE[123]	DESCRIPTION (Subtypes)	SIMILAR
DISTRIBUTIVE (Aristotle)	Getting one's *fair share* (allocation of goods and anything else in society)	**ATTRIBUTIVE** (Grotius): fitting, suitable allotments based on moral (not legal) obligations, or on a status, or skill (not legally enforceable; *imperfect* rights)

---

[123] As indicated, the first four kinds are classically Aristotle's, and I am comparing him mainly to Grotius and modern Social Justice, as they have similarities. *See Four Types of Justice*, CHANGING MINDS http://changingminds.org/explanations/trust/four_justice.htm (last visited May 5, 2019) (an introduction). Social Justice is a fairly new term, not in Aristotle's lexicon, but having similarities to some of Aristotle's and Grotius' kinds. Divine Justice is God's justice, in Christ or outside of Him. It's for individuals and nations, and includes temporal and eternal dimensions. It is a separate kind (not elaborated in this human-version chart, yet obvious in Scripture). Several other classifications exist by other scholars. I have chosen not to include them in this short table.

TYPE	DESCRIPTION (Subtypes)	SIMILAR
PROCEDURAL (Aristotle)	Getting a *fair process* (due process)	
RETRIBUTIVE (Aristotle)	Punishment, consequences for crimes, wrongs	
RESTORATIVE/ (Aristotle) **CORRECTIVE** (= *Rectification* or *Restitution*); incl., *'Commutative'*	Fixing wrongs in either *involuntary 'transactions'* [situations] (crimes, injuries), or in *voluntary transactions* (i.e., *Contracts*, commercial dealings; voluntary = Aristotle's **Commutative** justice)	**EXPLETIVE** (Grotius); based on legal rights (i.e. contracts, property ownership, repairs to injuries, etc.), that one actually has and can legally enforce (*perfect/complete* rights)
SOCIAL (New, not Aristotle)	Has biblical & non-biblical versions: i) improper wealth redistribution = non-biblical **Distributive**; ii) appropriate care of needy= biblical	**DISTRIBUTIVE, ATTRIBUTIVE** (similarities with Social Justice) i) non-biblical = equality of shares; ii) biblical = closer to **Corrective**

APPENDIX III

A Sample Working List of Human Rights
Seen in Various Christian Traditions[124]

A Basic List

As humans, we have rights *to life; liberty; property (to own, use, and steward it)* – (these 3 are at the top of most lists)*; to the pursuit of happiness* (see U.S. Declaration of Independence)*; to work (to provide for ourselves and families, to be creative, and to pursue calling); to use and develop one's intellect and mind (education); to have sustenance for life, including basic necessities such as food, clothing, shelter; to marry (and to enjoy marital fidelity); to have and raise a family (to educate and train one's children, including for economic pursuits); to security of one's person, property and possessions (including their safety); to enjoy basic human freedoms like thought (opinion), conscience, religion (including but not limited to worship), to speech, assembly, association, press, travel (movement, freedom from undue restriction of it); to good reputation (freedom from slander); to enjoy freedoms from slavery, cruelty in punishment, and torture* (but torture is controversial both as to definition and in some applications, including imminent terrorist threats)*; to enjoy non-discrimination in society of these basic human rights* (i.e., enjoyment is not based on inherent human characteristics such as race, ethnicity, color, sex)*; to equal protection and treatment under the law* (i.e., such is available to all citizens)*; to due process of law (including the right to be heard, fair trials, and fair criminal and civil procedures); to participate and be heard in government (representation, a right to address grievances, etc.)*

Some rights are *waivable,* and some may be *forfeited,* and some *are not.* For instance, a right to freedom of movement can be forfeited by jail time due to a valid criminal conviction. So can a right to life. Some rights inhere all through one's life, and some do not, but spring into effect only in certain conditions;

---

[124] The primary source of this compilation is the survey of rights in JOHN WITTE, JR., GOD'S JOUST, GOD'S JUSTICE, LAW AND RELIGION IN THE WESTERN TRADITION 38, 40, 45-46, 72, 81-82, 84, 93 (2006).

e.g., a right to *marry* or to a *fair trial* does not apply to a one-year-old child (such rights that spring into effect and have relevance only at certain times or in certain situations can be called *conditional rights*).[125] A right to be free from "slavery" does not apply to a prisoner of war from an aggressor nation; that is a *forfeiture* (although other rights of humane treatment should apply). Similarly, some exceptions to torture may be necessary (ticking time bombs, etc.). But a right to a fair hearing or trial is non-waivable (even if a trial does not go forward), but the right to a trial itself can be *waived* (in favor of arbitration, e.g.), and a jury trial can sometimes be waived in favor of a judge (bench) trial. Justice calls for wisdom in these situations (Proverbs 8).

Other ways of sorting rights into categories are shown in the table below.

Common Ways of Sorting Subjective Rights[a]

Common Vocabulary and Contrasts in Kinds of Rights [b]	Explanations [c]
Public (Constitutional) vs. Private (Personal)	what an individual or group should be guaranteed from his/their government (see also Civil below)
	man to man, person to person, including some entities having legal personality: the contract example in the text, as well as rights of an injured slip and fall victim in a store, a right to choose your child's schooling, your spouse, and religion, inheritance, and private and exclusive property rights are common examples

---

[125] This expression comes from Timothy Endicott. *See* Wolterstorff, *supra* note 18, at 18 (discussing Endicott's idea). Others disagree with it, and say either we have these rights or don't, so that an individual has rights to marry, to a fair trial, and so on, whether or not s/he ever gets to use them (is ever married or in court). *Id.* at 18-20. In any case, some rights always seem to be active, like *freedom of conscience*, while others sit idle.

Common Vocabulary and Contrasts in Kinds of Rights [b]	Explanations [c]
Human vs.	rights we have just for being human; includes life, liberty, and property; in turn, liberty includes "fundamental freedoms" (of speech, religion, assembly, association, press, movement); security in one's person and possessions, etc.; but see expansion in types of so-called 1st (political and civil 'fundamental'), 2nd (economic, social, cultural), and 3rd (environmental, developmental, and 'peace') generations of rights, criticized in the text
Civil vs.	what an individual gets expressly for being a citizen of a nation, as expressed often in a Constitution and Civil Rights Statutes (see also Public above)
Legal	those protected by law, including many of those otherwise mentioned herein, including Private legal rights (contracts, etc. above); a State imposed sanction protecting the rights is the important feature
Individual vs.	those inhering in individuals
Associations or Groups (Collective)	those of any private groups, businesses, religious associations, or public ones like cities and agencies
Natural vs.	those based on Natural Law, fundamental Human Rights
Positive	those issued by a State's positive law (enacted); and it may (should not) differ from Natural Rights
Inalienable vs.	those human rights which really can't be waived, or can be only in rare cases as required in law (life, and liberty, such as for capital crimes, or a need to incarcerate someone for a crime)
Alienable	waivable rights, like the right of an accused individual to remain silent, or to a jury trial

Common Vocabulary and Contrasts in Kinds of Rights [b]	Explanations [c]
Substantive vs.	can include fundamental rights and substantive legal and other rights in categories above, if distinct from Procedural
Procedural	rights to due process and other fair processes (jury trial, right to confront witnesses, right against self-incrimination, various administrative rights)
Imperfect (vs.)	a true right, and basic need of someone exists, but without a specific, matching, legally-imposed duty by the State on someone in particular to satisfy it (someone has to do it; Good Samaritans) (Wolterstorff, 2010)
Conditional	the idea is some rights exist but are not yet applicable, and actualized until certain conditions arise; a right to vote means nothing to a 1-yr-old (Endicott, 2010); others, in contrast, say not a right at all, not even an imperfect one (Wolterstorff, 2010)

Table Notes.

a) Categories are drawn largely from WITTE, *supra* note 124, at 32.

b) A right can fit into more than one category; the right to marry and have a family is a *human right*, a *legal right*, a *personal right*, and in many states, a *constitutional* and a *civil right*.

c) Similar to, yet distinct from rights, are the concepts of *privileges* (where a special status of a person gives her a right to do or not do something that another kind of person doesn't have), and *immunities* (a kind of right to avoid a consequence someone else would not normally have). Privileges and immunities also function in the domain of justice. *See* WITTE, *supra* note 124.

APPENDIX IV

Summary of Secular and
Christian Theories of Law (Table 4.1)[i]

Theory/ Proponents	Definition	Source of Law	Its Characteristics	Valid Strengths	Valid Criticisms
Scripture, Qualified Theonomy v. **Reconstructionism** (in varying degrees) [ii] / Proponents: Greg Bahnsen Gary North Rousas Rushdooney	God's Word, Scripture applied as civil law in society in context appropriate ways v. Legalistic literalism	Scripture; Special (Written) Revelation, and how it should be interpreted (some reasoning is used casuistically – not "source")	- 10 Commandments & Casuistry (illustrations, cases); - The Laws in Scripture for Israel apply sometimes by analogy or for their broader **Principles** [e.g., restitution is great but we restore a car's value, not usually an ox's]; or, Israel's laws strictly apply to all countries at all times [not the favored view]; - Key words in Hebrew for Justice: *tsedeq* (doing right), *mishpat* (judicially right), *hesed* (love, mercy) - Distinctions between **Moral, Civil,** and **Ceremonial** laws are vital. (What did Jesus, or NT keep and change, and how much is for all humanity in all times?) [iii] 1) **Moral Law:** Continues, 10 Commandments (right and wrong), but context is important 2) **Civil Law:** Cases, justice system, does not have to be exactly as Israel's, analogy, Principles 3) **Ceremonial Law:** Jesus/NT changed: circumcision, sacrificial system is over - Two Approaches on continuation: a) **Maintained unless Modified** (Moral and Civil, not Ceremonial); b) **Repealed unless Repeated** - *What is valid outside of Israel is valid since Israel. (J. Kirkaola)*	Some Principles and Laws of Scripture are Universal; **10 Commandments** (see last 5) All law is based on moral, religious views of some kind	Over – literalistic; sometimes lack of a clear hermeneutic for application today [stoning our kids for back talk vs. applying a General Principle: respecting authority]; *Theonomy* is called a fringe by some, but is not the same as strict Reconstructionism, and this claim skirts the issue of valid applications

Theory/Proponents	Definition	Source of Law	Its Characteristics	Valid Strengths	Valid Criticisms
Natural Law (Christian)/ Augustine, Aquinas, Luther, Calvin, Blackstone, CS Lewis, America's Founding Fathers, Finnis, Hittinger, Locke, Grotius, D'Entreves, Van Drunen, S. Graybill	Unwritten law inside humans as created in Image of God; knowledge of Right vs. Wrong is inside; in our Conscience; Blackstone called it: the **Will of the Maker**; God's moral will revealed to all man generally, internally	God via General Revelation; Inside you, in the inner man, heart, conscience, but placed there by God at and with His creation of us	- It should never contradict Scripture, since it is the Will of God, generally revealed - It predates Scripture, and can be used with and alongside Scripture, and Scripture clarifies its vagaries [iv] - It is unwritten, but can be put into writing or expressed verbally; in your conscience - It explains how even fallen, corrupted humans can have any capacity to make good laws for the benefit of others (laws against rape, sex-trafficking, larceny, enforcing Ks); - It relies on sound reason for its apprehension (reason is not the source of this law, God is; reason is a mechanism of seeing it); Sound reasoning is also used to apply general moral principles, so perceived, to specific situations (some equate it too much w/reason) [v] - It is instructive on the most basic human norms; a distinction must be made between conclusions (universals) and determinations (varying in contexts); e.g., safety in NL (conclusion), but which side of the street to drive on is variable (determination) - Human consensus on a moral principle is also not = NL, but can be evidence of it	It's already in you (in your conscience); it is used all the time in everyday affairs (even with Scripture); It helps convict of wrongdoing; Since every human being has some (Imago Dei), there is always some moral substance to work with in all humans; NL is supported by sound logic and thinking; it explains how humans legislate	Due to sin, people make improper moral judgments all the time [although they can also make proper ones] (People can be easily deceived, or intentionally in rebellion). It is easily confused with *secular Enlightenment rationalism* (it is not that). Content is vague beyond very basic norms (unreliable); Rely on Scripture in a conflict. It can be influenced, rightly or *wrongly* (as in conscience)

Theory/ Proponents	Definition	Source of Law	Its Characteristics	Valid Strengths	Valid Criticisms
			- International norms: *jus cogens* , *jus gentium* (Customary International Law: 'CIL'), Other Int'l custom, and *jus civile* [vi] - It can be informed, instructed, increased in individuals; moral reasoning can be used to convince people about right and wrong (moral reasoning is possible, if not always successful) see Acts 24:25 (discussion with Paul and Felix) - It judges man, and points to the need of a Savior since people cannot live up to it. - It cannot cancel man's sin nature; it can't save anyone - It helps people govern - It is in Christians and non-Christians (in humans), yet seen in varying degrees		

133

Theory/ Proponents	Definition	Source of Law	Its Characteristics	Valid Strengths	Valid Criticisms
Positivism/ Jeremy Bentham, John Austin, Hans Kelsen, H.L.A. Hart	What the State enacts as law, at its various levels of authority, is law: "imperatives emanating from the government" (J. Brauch)	The State, humans (legislators, judges, civil administrators)	- Law is valid if it comes from the properly designated State instrumentality. Moral content is not a serious consideration - Law is not necessarily devoid of moral substance (substantive norms), but Kelsen ignores this in the *Pure Theory of Law* to look at its more important procedural validity (the norms of its making); is law coming from the properly constituted authority? - A scientific approach (analysis) on how that basic law-making norm is accomplished - Is generally opposed to NL, not necessarily because it is wrong, but more through marginalization; NL (morality) seen as significantly less important - Importance of what IS the law over what it OUGHT to be	How we make laws, in following established basic procedural norms, is very important. Law is hierarchical in society	Extracting or Ignoring the moral component of law was a really bad idea (Nazi Germany showed this). Largely discredited; And not all legal systems are the same (Positivism is too Western)

Theory/ Proponents	Definition	Source of Law	Its Characteristics	Valid Strengths	Valid Criticisms
Realism; Sociological-Historical (earlier branches)// Holmes (precursor), Llewelyn, Roscoe Pound (Sociological Branch), Cardozo	Law is what the judge says it is, not what the judge *says s/ he is doing*; it varies, is uncertain. (1920s to 1930s heyday)	Judges, their biases, ideas and beliefs; NOT pre-existing fixed moral norms or rules; is against NL and **Legal Formalism:** Idea of applying specific laws in cases	- Skeptical of moral law and moral reasoning. A reaction to **Legal Formalism**, with its emphasis on applying legal rules (norms), via logical deduction, to the facts, in order to determine cases; Critical of NL and notions of *a priori truths*. - Instead or legal rules, facts of cases is what is important in determining outcomes, including how such facts are assessed, 'interpreted,' and categorized by jurists; some comparisons in a case with other cases is inevitable, but judges often decide according to their own preferred visions on social, and public policy issues (their vision of social welfare). - Critical of the idea judges "find" the law in a case; instead, judges **make** the law in a case - Cynical: looking at how judges often do what they want, based on their personal influences, and not often on fixed principles; decisions are more like "rationalizations." [vii] – A situation of the *Is*, versus the *Ought*, in legal systems, again - Jurisprudence is about predicting what the judge will do; and skill in this - Legislatively too, law makers are constantly appeasing special interests; Is it even Law?	Sad but true, judicial decisions often don't follow legal principles. Facts are indeed important: cases are decided by analogizing, or distinguishing facts from case precedents, and Law does have a *factual context* (but still is Law); in some sense, judges do make law	What is sometimes done in the name of "law," in result, is really not law at all. Situation of *Is vs. Ought*; Legal Realism may be more Descriptive than Prescriptive. Law is still law, even if not properly followed. Law can't be and isn't actually ignored by most jurists. Law guides their decisions. In most cases, judges do apply the correct law, and can easily do so - Loose label, as Realists often disagreed with each other, except on essentials

Theory/Proponents	Definition	Source of Law	Its Characteristics	Valid Strengths	Valid Criticisms
			- Inspired most recent schools of Critical Legal Studies, Critical Race Theory, Feminist Jurisprudence, Gay Jurisprudence, Law & Economics (all said to be offshoots of Realism). "We are all realists now." (see J. Brauch) - Has **Sociological** jurisprudence sides, as in social engineering (R. Pound) [viii]		
Critical Legal Studies/ R. Unger, D. Kennedy, M. Kelman, R. Gordon	There is no law, only politics (1970s – 1990s)	n/a: "laws" are merely enactments of those in power to achieve their agendas, and protect their elitist interests	- Critical means it takes apart the façade of what is called law and looks at the underlying ideologies, exposing actual value assumptions behind the law, revealing power politics - Hidden ideologies, nothing is neutral, none is superior, some ideologies should also be fought against as oppressive; Can have neo-Marxist influences; Deconstruction, Trashing of world views[x] - It is seen as a mostly defunct school now, but has branched into more other specific applications: Critical Race Theory, Feminist, and Gay Jurisprudence.	It's true those in power tend to make laws advancing their interests; hidden ideologies, and systemic injustices, are sometimes indeed revealed	This is what is really happening, but this is not what should be happening; it's not the whole story either. Some law exists and is valid. CLS suffers from its own critique of ideological views

Theory/ Proponents	Definition	Source of Law	Its Characteristics	Valid Strengths	Valid Criticisms
Critical Race Theory/ D. Bell, Barnes, R. Delgado, A. Mutua (1989)	Law is explained as a reflection of race struggle	Not really law, but the politics of the powerful and oppressive	- Critical of the idea of law - Power of the oppressor to serve its own self-interests at the expense of the weaker minority - African American injustice was original focus of criticism in America - Lat Crit (Latino/latina critical studies) and other racial injustice focuses have also now emerged (American issues)	Some of it is true historically	Again, situation of what sometimes *is*, not what *ought* to be law; too limiting to explain all law this way; subject to the same self-critique of ideology as in CLS
Feminist Jurisprudence + Gay Jurisprudence/ A.C. Scales, K.Crenshaw	Law is explained as a reflection of gender or sexual orientation struggle	Not really law, but the politics of the powerful and oppressive	- Same idea - Same but as to gender and sexual orientation issues - **Gay Jurisprudence** subsequently arrived, examining legal systems and power struggles perceived as intolerant of so-called *gay rights*, - **Transgender Identity** issues are now shaping jurisprudence and rights conversations	Same issues	Same issues Transgender ideas, with gender fluidity and supposedly many genders, conflicts with binary sex and gender structure in Gay (M-M; F-F) and Feminist (F-M) jurisprudence; thus creating internal conflicts within LGBTQI jurisprudence

Theory/ Proponents	Definition	Source of Law	Its Characteristics	Valid Strengths	Valid Criticisms
Law & Economics/ Richard Posner, R. Coase, G. Calebresi	Law is explained primarily (essentially) as economic decision-making (costs, and risk analysis) (1960s - 70s – Present)	Man, mainly Jurists and Economists	- Asserts laws, including judicial decisions, are based on economics: cost-benefit analysis in making laws and in judicial decisions (i.e., damage awards and calculations) - Ultimate social goal is wealth maximization (= social welfare idea, different than Scriptural idea) - Economic analysis can be both at the society level, or individual case level - Efficiency of economic resources is stressed - Wealth maximization is seen as a good normative idea for society (makes people better off, and not as poor); some K *breaches* are said to achieve that; has *normative* as well as *descriptive* approaches. - *Utilitarian* - Efficient breach of K is one of its more questionable tenets (Psalm 15:4, Keeping one's word is important, even if it is painful; calculate your bargain)	Efficiency is a good thing; wealth maximization in society is a good goal in itself (it should reduce poverty); is realistic and pragmatic	1) Wealth maximization at the expense of individual justice in a given case is not good; 2) Efficient breach of K, encourages breaches, erodes trust (if one can do it, all can); 3) criticized for saying law is all economics; 4) and for suggesting repugnant ideas: adoptable babies as commodities to sell; 5) seen as sometimes inhumane, cold.

Theory/Proponents	Definition	Source of Law	Its Characteristics	Valid Strengths	Valid Criticisms
			- Has become the dominant school of jurisprudence in the last decade (or most talked about); considered conservative by some due to market economics approach to legal systems. - Is interpreted sometimes as putting money above justice (sometimes this happens, and L & E attempts to justify some casualties, for the wealth of society as a whole; cf. *Captain America* II; *Kaldor-Hicks* efficiency standard) - Sometimes unfeeling, inhumane sounding (i.e., justifying selling adoptable babies as commodities);		

[i] Secular theories may embody some truth in them but are incomplete in themselves. Some have aspects antithetical to Christianity. The first two categories in the Table present the most comprehensive, biblical acknowledgment of moral truth in law. The remaining theories often describe what is going on in law, and in some cases prescribe a course for the law, and show a mix of some useful and some harmful ideas. A tension can exist between what *Is* in Law, and what it *Ought* to be.

[ii] The term *Theocracy* is often incorrectly applied here to what I call *Qualified Theonomy*, or to its extreme, *Reconstructionism*. *Theocracy* is the direct rule of God as King over His people (Israel). In a broad sense of God's Sovereignty, it may refer to His rule over every nation, since there isn't an inch of the Universe God does not ultimately reign over as Supreme (Kuyper). The term cannot refer to the use of religious values to shape or inform a country's laws, since laws are inherently infused and shaped by religious and moral values in cultures, anyway.

[iii] This 3-part structure is often associated with Christ's 3 roles as Prophet (Moral law), Priest (Ceremonial, religious law), and King (Civil law). Law in each the prophetic, and kingly roles has greater continuity in NT, but no so in the priestly role, since Jesus clearly abolished the Jewish sacrificial system and is our High Priest. Civil ideals like equity, honest judging, and due process continue, sometimes as analogous principles from the OT for today, even if not applied in exactly the same way as in Israel.

[iv] Scripture does not eliminate the need for NL, since Scripture does not answer every moral dilemma in human history. One sometimes has to reason from the general principles (GPs) in Scripture (or from NL with its general morality, as still consistent with Scripture), and apply the GPs to particular contexts. Is killing someone in self-defense a violation of Scripture? (No), but what verses answer this question fully without some thinking and comparisons? Is borrowing the company car to take someone to the hospital in an emergency situation against Scripture when the car is generally not allowed for any personal use? Scripture, its General Principles, and the NL each provide general substantive moral norms from which we must reason and apply, in specific contexts, to get right answers (in some cases, however, this is not so easy to do).

[v] Some people equate NL with human reason. This is incorrect. Reason is a process involved in NL's apprehension. Human reason, however, must be morally informed and guided, and should follow certain rules. In this confusion of terms, some scholars have historically used *Reason* as something morally imbued (something *good*); if they do that, they are not indicating simple human reasoning, independent of God, as it is sometimes used today (*see* Augustine, Aquinas).

^{vi} Each of these corresponds with parts of the Natural Law: *Jus Cogens* (Conclusions), *Jus Gentium* (Conclusions), Other International Customary Law(s) – Regional, etc. (Conclusions, Determinations), *Jus Civile* (Conclusions, Determinations).

^{vii} **Public Choice Theory** is a derivative of this school (especially of Holmes), seeing legislation as mostly an award going to the highest bidder among special interest groups (several such cases are documented). *See* Albert W. Alschuler, *A Century of Skepticism, in* CHRISTIAN PERSPECTIVES ON LEGAL THOUGHT 94, 97 (Michael W. McConnell, Robert F. Cochran, Jr., Angela C. Carmella eds., 2001).

^{viii} I have included **Sociological - Historical Jurisprudence** here in **Realism**, since social engineering (i.e., that judges should seek to influence some social welfare or agendas in cases, instead of just applying the law) is a central theme in Realism. Social engineering in Realism has led to a vibrant debate on *judicial activism v. conservative judging.* An earlier and different kind of Sociological Jurisprudence (less agendized), sprang out of Historical Jurisprudence (norms seen in a society through its cultural, historical lenses), and taught that law emanates through the social norms, and cultural and religious practices of a society, based on shared values, over time (Savigny), and so was more consistent with a Natural Law approach (shared moral customs, and norms in a society), than what we now associate with judicial activism and social engineering (i.e., sociological jurisprudence currently).

^{ix} This critique can be more moderate, as an attempt to unmask all these hidden assumptions and ideologies, or more revolutionary in its approach to change (to liberate from oppression). The same holds true for the offshoots of Critical Race, and Feminist Jurisprudence; and still another offshoot is Gay Jurisprudence. Thus, often these are called *Deconstructionist* theories. *Trashing* is part of the strategy.

APPENDIX V

Scriptures From Proverbs on Good Governance

1. Proverbs 8:15. *By me kings reign and rulers issue decrees that are just . . . .*
2. Proverbs 11:10. *When the righteous prosper, the city rejoices; when the wicked perish, there are shouts of joy.*
3. Proverbs 14:34. *Righteousness exalts a nation, but sin condemns any people.*
4. Proverbs 14:35. *A king delights in a wise servant, but a shameful servant arouses his fury.*
5. Proverbs 16:10. *The lips of a king speak as an oracle, and his mouth does not betray justice.*
6. Proverbs 16:12. *Kings detest wrongdoing, for a throne is established through righteousness.*
7. Proverbs 16:13. *Kings take pleasure in honest lips; they value the one who speaks what is right.*
8. Proverbs 16:14. *A king's wrath is a messenger of death, but the wise will appease it.*
9. Proverbs 16:15. *When a king's face brightens, it means life; his favor is like a rain cloud in spring. A king's rage is like the roar of a lion, but his favor is like dew on the grass.*
10. Proverbs 18:12. *Before a downfall the heart is haughty, but humility comes before honor.*
11. Proverbs 19:10: *It is not fitting for a fool to live in luxury— how much worse for a slave to rule over princes!*
12. Proverbs 19:12. *A king's rage is like the roar of a lion, but his favor is like dew on the grass.*
13. Proverbs 20:2. *A king's wrath strikes terror like the roar of a lion; those who anger him forfeit their lives.*
14. Proverbs 20:8. *When a king sits on his throne to judge, he winnows out all evil with his eyes.*

15. Proverbs 20:26. *A wise king winnows out the wicked; he drives the threshing wheel over them.*
16. Proverbs 20:28. *Love and faithfulness keep a king safe; through love his throne is made secure.*
17. Proverbs 21:1. *In the Lord's hand the king's heart is a stream of water that he channels toward all who please him.*
18. Proverbs 21:22. *One who is wise can go up against the city of the mighty and pull down the stronghold in which they trust.*
19. Proverbs 22:7. *The rich rule over the poor, and the borrower is slave to the lender.*
20. Proverbs 22:11. *One who loves a pure heart and who speaks with grace will have the king for a friend.*
21. Proverbs 22:29. *Do you see someone skilled in their work? They will serve before kings; they will not serve before officials of low rank.*
22. Proverbs 24:21. *Fear the Lord and the king, my son, and do not join with rebellious officials,*
23. Proverbs 25:5. *[R]emove wicked officials from the king's presence, and his throne will be established through righteousness.*
24. Proverbs 27:24. *[F]or riches do not endure forever, and a crown is not secure for all generations.*
25. Proverbs 28:2. *When a country is rebellious, it has many rulers, but a ruler with discernment and knowledge maintains order.*
26. Proverbs 28:3. *A ruler who oppresses the poor is like a driving rain that leaves no crops.*
27. Proverbs 28:12. *When the righteous triumph, there is great elation; but when the wicked rise to power, people go into hiding.*
28. Proverbs 28:15. *Like a roaring lion or a charging bear is a wicked ruler over a helpless people.*
29. Proverbs 28:16. *A tyrannical ruler practices extortion, but one who hates ill-gotten gain will enjoy a long reign.*
30. Proverbs 28:28. *When the wicked rise to power, people go into hiding; but when the wicked perish, the righteous thrive.*
31. Proverbs 29:2. *When the righteous thrive, the people rejoice; when the wicked rule, the people groan.*

32. Proverbs 29:4. *By justice a king gives a country stability, but those who are greedy for bribes tear it down.*
33. Proverbs 29:12. *If a ruler listens to lies, all his officials become wicked.*
34. Proverbs 29:14. *If a king judges the poor with fairness, his throne will be established forever.*
35. Proverbs 29:26. *Many seek an audience with a ruler, but it is from the Lord that one gets justice.*

APPENDIX VI

Scripture Verses on Bribery and Injustice

Scripture verses on Bribery (**emphasis** is the author's)

1. Exodus 23:8. *Do not accept a **bribe**, for a bribe blinds those who see and twists the words of the innocent.*

2. Deuteronomy 10:17. *For the LORD your God is God of gods and Lord of lords, the great God, mighty and awesome, who shows no partiality and accepts no **bribes.***

3. Deuteronomy 16:19. *Do not pervert justice or show partiality. Do not accept a **bribe**, for a **bribe** blinds the eyes of the wise and twists the words of the innocent.*

4. Deuteronomy 27:25. *Cursed is anyone who accepts a **bribe** to kill an innocent person.*

5. 1 Samuel 8:3. *But his sons did not follow his ways. They turned aside after dishonest gain and accepted **bribes** and perverted justice.*

6. 1 Samuel 12:3. *Here I stand. Testify against me in the presence of the LORD and his anointed. Whose ox have I taken? Whose donkey have I taken? Whom have I cheated? Whom have I oppressed? From whose hand have I accepted a **bribe** to make me shut my eyes? If I have done any of these things, I will make it right.*

7. 2 Chronicles 19:7. *Now let the fear of the LORD be on you. Judge carefully, for with the LORD our God there is no injustice or partiality or **bribery.***

8. Ezra 4:5. *They **bribed** officials to work against them and frustrate their plans during the entire reign of Cyrus king of Persia and down to the reign of Darius king of Persia.*

9. Job 15:34. *For the company of the godless will be barren, and fire will consume the tents of those who love **bribes.***

10. Job 36:18. *Be careful that no one entices you by riches; do not let a large **bribe** turn you aside.*

11. Psalm 15:5. *who lends money to the poor without interest; who does not accept a **bribe** against the innocent. Whoever does these things will never be shaken.*

12. Psalm 17:4. *Though people tried to **bribe** me, I have kept myself from the ways of the violent through what your lips have commanded.*

13. Psalm 26:10. *in whose hands are wicked schemes, whose right hands are full of **bribes**.*

14. Proverbs 6:35. *He will not accept any compensation; he will refuse a **bribe**, however great it is.*

15. Proverbs 15:27. *The greedy bring ruin to their households, but the one who hates **bribes** will live.*

16. Proverbs 17:8. *A **bribe** is seen as a charm by the one who gives it; they think success will come at every turn.*

17. Proverbs 17:23. *The wicked accept **bribes** in secret to pervert the course of justice.*

18. Proverbs 21:14. *A gift given in secret soothes anger, and a **bribe** concealed in the cloak pacifies great wrath.*

19. Proverbs 29:4. *By justice a king gives a country stability, but those who are greedy for **bribes** tear it down.*

20. Ecclesiastes 7:7. ***Extortion** turns a wise person into a fool, and a **bribe** corrupts the heart.*

21. Isaiah 1:23. *Your rulers are rebels, partners with thieves; they all love **bribes** and chase after gifts. They do not defend the cause of the fatherless; the widow's case does not come before them.*

22. Isaiah 5:23. *who acquit the guilty for a **bribe**, but deny justice to the innocent.*

23. Isaiah 33:15. *Those who walk righteously and speak what is right, who reject gain from **extortion** and keep their hands from accepting **bribes**, who stop their ears against plots of murder and shut their eyes against contemplating evil . . . .*

24. Ezekiel 22:12. *In you are people who accept **bribes** to shed blood; you take interest and make a profit from the poor. You extort unjust gain from your neighbors. And you have forgotten me, declares the Sovereign LORD.*

25. Amos 5:12. *For I know how many are your offenses and how great your sins. There are those who oppress the innocent and take **bribes** and deprive the poor of justice in the courts.*

26. Micah 3:11. *Her leaders judge for a **bribe**, her priests teach for a price, and her prophets tell fortunes for money. Yet they look for the LORD's support and say, "Is not the LORD among us? No disaster will come upon us."*

27. Micah 7:3. *Both hands are skilled in doing evil; the ruler demands gifts, the judge accepts **bribes**, the powerful dictate what they desire— they all conspire together.*

28. Acts 24:26. *At the same time he was hoping that Paul would offer him a **bribe**, so he sent for him frequently and talked with him.*

APPENDIX VII

Links to Additional Resources
in The Text

The following charts and resources were mentioned in the main text above, and are available on the Advocates International ICLS/Resources page, at this address: https://resources.advocatesinternational.org/ai-resources.

Annotated Table 2.1 The annotated version of the chart, *A Taxonomy of Justice and Rights by Actions*, with over 10 pages of explanatory notes and illustrations.

Essay 8.1 *Historical Christian Views on Separation of Church and State*, with diagrams on several denominations' views on the issue of separation (6 pp.).

Slide 11.1 Slide-diagram and explanation illustrating a self-feeding cycle of corruption and poverty, causing increasing social ills in communities, through corruption at both the national (macro) and local/community (micro) levels.

Slide 11.2 Slide-diagram and explanation illustrating corruption in both administrative (bureaucratic), and public justice (criminal) law systems, as impacting the developing world.

Slides 12.1 PowerPoint illustrating four approaches of Christian attorneys in current practice (Allegretti's framework), with additional input.

Made in United States
Orlando, FL
14 January 2023

28679833R00091